P9-CRQ-832

MARRIAGE UNDER FIRE

DR. JAMES DOBSON

MARRIAGE UNDER FIRE

WHY WE **MUST** WIN THIS WAR

Multnomah® Publishers *Sisters, Oregon*

MARRIAGE UNDER FIRE
published by Multnomah Publishers, Inc.

International Standard Book Number: 1-59052-431-4

Cover design by Kirk DouPonce/UDG DesignWorks, Inc.

Printed in the United States of America

For information:
MULTNOMAH PUBLISHERS, INC. • P.O. BOX 1720 • SISTERS, OR 97759

Library of Congress Cataloging-in-Publication Data

Dobson, James C., 1936-
Marriage under fire : why we must win this war / James C. Dobson.
p. cm.
Includes bibliographical references.
ISBN 1-59052-431-4
1. Marriage—United States. 2. Family—United States. 3. Marriage law—United States. 4. Social values—United States. I. Title.

HQ536.D62 2004
306.81'0973—dc22

2004009830

04 05 06 07 08 09 10—10 9 8 7 6 5 4 3 2 1 0

CONTENTS

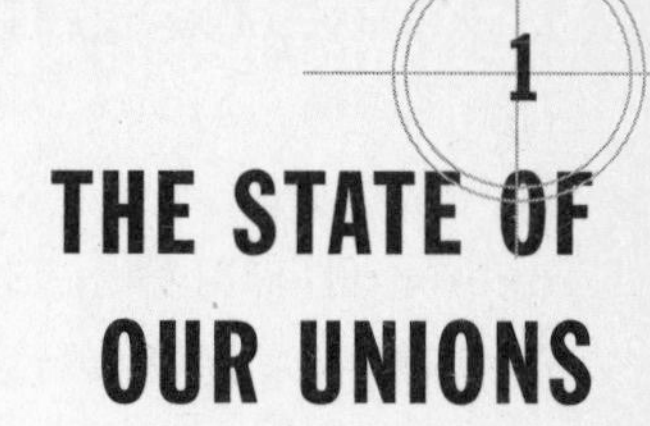

1 THE STATE OF OUR UNIONS

Behold, the institution of marriage! It is one of the Creator's most marvelous and enduring gifts to humankind. This divine plan was revealed to Adam and Eve in the Garden of Eden and then described succinctly in Genesis 2:24, where we read, "Therefore shall a man leave his father and his mother, and shall cleave unto his wife: and they shall be one flesh" (KJV). With those twenty-two words, God announced the ordination of the family, long before He established the two other great human institutions, the church and the government.

Five thousand years of recorded history have come and gone, yet every civilization in the history of the world has been built upon it.[1] Despite today's skeptics, who claim that marriage is an outmoded and narrow-minded Christian concoction, the desire of men and women to "leave" and "cleave" has survived and thrived through times of prosperity, peace, famine, wars, epidemics, and every other possible circumstance and condition. It has been the bedrock of culture in Asia, Africa, Europe, North America, South America, Australia, and even Antarctica. Given this unbroken continuity, one might begin to suspect that something mystical within human nature must be drawing the sexes together—not just for purposes of reproduction as with animals, but to satisfy an irrepressible longing for companionship, intimacy, and spiritual bonding. Indeed, how can it be doubted? Passion finds its fulfillment in the institution of marriage.

Admittedly, there have been periods in history when homosexuality has flourished, as in the biblical cities of Sodom and Gomorrah, in ancient Greece, and in the Roman Empire. None of these civilizations survived. Furthermore, even where sexual perversion was tolerated, marriage continued to be honored in law and custom.

Only in the last few years have two countries, the Netherlands and Belgium, actually legalized what is called "gay marriage" and given it equal status with traditional male-female unions.[2] The impact of that vast sociological experiment is no longer speculative. We can see where it leads by observing the Scandinavian nations of Norway, Denmark, and Sweden, whose leaders embraced de facto marriages between homosexuals in the nineties. The consequences for traditional families have been devastating. The institution of marriage in those countries is rapidly dying, with most young couples cohabiting or choosing to remain single. In some areas of Norway, 80 percent of firstborn children are conceived out of wedlock, as are 60 percent of subsequent births.[3] It appears that tampering with the ancient plan for males and females spells doom for the family and for everything related to it. We will consider why this is true in a subsequent chapter.

To put it succinctly, the institution of marriage represents the very foundation of human social order. Everything of value sits on that base. Institutions, governments, religious fervor, and the welfare of children are all dependent on its stability. When it is weakened or undermined, the entire superstructure begins to wobble. That is exactly what has happened during the last thirty-five years, as radical feminists, liberal lawmakers, and profiteers in the entertainment industry have taken their toll on the stability of marriage. Many of our pressing social problems can be traced to this origin.

MADE FOR EACH OTHER

One reason the preservation of the family is critical to the health of nations is the enormous influence the sexes have on each other. They are specifically designed to "fit" together, both physically and emotionally, and neither is entirely comfortable without the other. There are exceptions, of course, but this is the norm. George Gilder, the brilliant sociologist and author of the book *Men and Marriage,* states that women hold *the* key to the stability and productivity of men.[4] When a wife believes in her husband and deeply respects him, he gains the confidence necessary to compete successfully and live responsibly. She gives him a reason to harness his masculine energy—to build a home, obtain and keep a job, help her raise their children, remain sober, live within the law, spend money wisely, etc. Without positive feminine influence, his tendency is to release the power of testosterone in a way that is destructive to himself and to society at large.

We see Gilder's insight played out in the inner city. Our welfare system, in the aftermath of the Great Society programs, rendered millions of men superfluous. Indeed, government assistance to women and children was reduced or denied when a father was present in the home. Food stamps put groceries in the pantry. The Department of Housing and Urban Development sent repairmen to fix maintenance problems. When children were in trouble, social workers stepped in to help. Thus men became unnecessary beyond the act of impregnation. Who needed 'em? Gilder contends that this disengagement with women and their children explains why drug abuse, alcoholism, crime, and absentee fathers have been rampant in inner-city settings. Men were separated from their historic role as providers and protectors, which stripped them of masculine dignity and robbed them of meaning and purpose. Thus, as Gilder said, their energy became a destructive force instead of powering growth and personal development.[5]

Stated positively, a man is dependent for stability and direction on what he derives from a woman, which is why the bonding that occurs between the sexes is so important to society at large. Successful marriages serve to "civilize" and domesticate masculinity, which is not only in the best interests of women, but is vital for the protection and welfare of the next generation.

Conversely, a woman typically has deep longings that can only be satisfied through a romantic, long-term relationship with a man. Her self-esteem, contentment, and fulfillment are typically derived from intimacy, heart-to-heart, in marriage. Unfortunately, most young husbands find these emotional needs in their wives to be not only confusing, but downright baffling at times. That was certainly true of my early relationship with my wife, Shirley. It took me several years of marriage to "get it," and we experienced some bumps in the road while I was sorting things out.

The most eye-opening encounter between us occurred on our first Valentine's Day together, six months after we were married. It was something of a disaster. I had gone to the USC library that morning and spent eight or ten hours poring over dusty books and journals. I had forgotten that it was February 14.

What was worse, I was oblivious to the preparations that were going on at home. Shirley had cooked a wonderful dinner, baked a pink heart-shaped cake with "Happy Valentine's Day" written on the top, placed several red candles on the table, wrapped a small gift she had bought for me, and written a little love note on a greeting card. The stage was set. She would meet me at the front door with a kiss and a hug. But there I sat on the other side of Los Angeles, blissfully unaware of the storm gathering overhead.

About 8 P.M., I got hungry and ordered a hamburger at the University Grill. After eating, I moseyed out to where my Volkswagen was parked and headed toward home. Then I made a terrible mistake that I would regret for many moons: I stopped by to see my parents, who lived near the freeway. Mom greeted me warmly and served up a great slice of apple pie. That sealed my doom.

When I finally put my key in the lock at 10:00, I knew instantly that something was horribly wrong. (I'm very perceptive about subtleties like that.) The apartment was dark and all was deathly quiet. There on the table was a coagulated dinner still sitting in our best dishes and bowls. Half-burned candles stood cold and dark in their silver-plated holders. It appeared that I had forgotten something important. But what? Then I noticed the red and white decorations on the table. *Oh no!* I thought.

So there I stood in the semidarkness of our little living room, feeling like a creep. I didn't even have a Valentine's Day card, much less a thoughtful gift, for Shirley. No romantic thoughts had crossed my mind all day. I couldn't even pretend to want the dried-up food that sat before me. After a brief flurry of words and a few tears, Shirley went to bed and pulled the covers up around her ears. I would have given a thousand dollars for a true, plausible explanation for my thoughtlessness. But there just wasn't one. It didn't help to tell her, "I stopped by my mom's house for a piece of great apple pie. It was wonderful. You should've been there."

Fortunately, Shirley is not only a romantic lady, but she is a forgiving one, too. We talked about my insensitivity later that night and came to an understanding. I learned a big lesson that Valentine's Day and determined never to forget it. I'll bet, however, that I'm not the only brute who has underestimated the importance of February 14. There must be several million guys who can identify with my failures as a husband.

Once I understood how my wife differed from me—especially regarding romantic things—I began to get with the program. One day I came home from work and asked Shirley to join me for a date that I called "Old Haunts." I took her to many of the places we had visited when we were going together in college. We went to the Pasadena Playhouse, where we had seen a theater performance on our second date. We walked through the Farmers Market and then ate pizza at Micelle's Italian restaurant in Los Angeles. We strolled along hand in hand, reminiscing about times gone by. Then we ended the day at our favorite restaurant in Pasadena, which was famous for their cherry pie and coffee. It was a wonderful afternoon and evening together, and I assure you, Shirley loved it.

What I was beginning to understand in those early days were the ways my wife was uniquely crafted, and how I alone could meet her most important emotional needs. Shirley was also learning some new things about me. She observed that I needed her to respect me, to believe in me, and to listen to my hopes and dreams. Shirley said all the right things, not because she was trying to manipulate me, but because she clearly believed them. She would often tell me, "I am proud of you, and I'm glad to be part of your team. It is going to be exciting to see what God will do with us in the days ahead." The way she looked up to me gave me confidence—I was a student who had never really accomplished anything up to that point—and empowered me to take risks professionally and to reach for the sky. She was meeting a critical need for me, precisely in the way George Gilder described. I was then motivated to give Shirley what she needed from me.

We have now been married for more than forty years, and it has been a great ride. I can't imagine life without her, and she professes to feel the same about me. I know marriage doesn't always work that successfully, but that is the way it was intended to be. When the predominate needs of one sex go unmet or ignored by the other, something akin to "soul hunger" occurs. It cannot be explained by cultural influences that are learned in childhood, as some would have us believe. It is deeply rooted in the human personality. That observation was confirmed for me time and again in my professional work as a psychologist, where those same patterns were evident in couples with whom I was working. Though I would not have described it in these terms at the time, there was clearly a divine plan in human nature that suited men and women for one another.

HURTLING TOWARD GOMORRAH

In short, marriage, when it functions as intended, is good for everyone—for men, for women, for children, for the community, for the nation, and for the world. Marriage is the means by which the human race is propagated, and the means by which spiritual teaching is passed down through the generations. Research consistently shows that heterosexual married adults do better in virtually every measure of emotional and physical health than people who are divorced or never married. They live longer and have happier lives. They recover from illness more quickly, earn and save more money, are more reliable employees, suffer less stress, and are less likely to become victims of any kind of violence. They find the job of parenting more enjoyable, and they have more satisfying and fulfilling sex lives. These and countless other benefits of marriage serve to validate (although no validation is necessary) the wisdom of the Creator, who told us what was best for mankind. He said in the book of Genesis, "It is not good for the man to be alone" (2:18). So he made Adam a helpmate, a partner, a lover—and then commanded them to "be fruitful and multiply" (9:7, NASB).

What a great plan. We depart from it at our peril.

A life in keeping with God's design and instruction brings the greatest possible fulfillment, while any deviation from His design invites disaster. This is why the Bible warns against all harmful forms of sexual behavior, including premarital sex, adultery, prostitution, incest, bestiality, and pedophilia. Homosexuality is only one of the several ways we can wound ourselves and devastate those around us. Ironically, homosexual activists strive with all their energies to achieve "freedom" from the shackles of moral law and traditional institutions. But the Scripture teaches that true freedom and genuine fulfillment can be found only when we live in harmony with our design.

The traditional family and marriage as defined from the dawn of time are among the few institutions that have, in fact, stood the test of time. If we now choose to stand idly by while these institutions are overthrown, the family as it has been known for millennia will be gone. And with its demise will come chaos such as the world has never seen before.

This is why I am profoundly concerned today about the effort to tamper with this time-honored institution. For nearly sixty years, the homosexual activist movement and related entities have been working to implement a master plan that has had as its centerpiece the utter destruction of the family.[6] Now the final battle is at hand: The institution of marriage and the Christian church are all that stand in the way of the movement's achievement of every coveted aspiration. Those goals include universal acceptance of the gay lifestyle, the discrediting of Scriptures that condemn homosexuality, muzzling of the clergy and Christian media, granting of special privileges and rights in the law, overturning laws prohibiting pedophilia, indoctrination of children and future generations through public education, and securing all the legal benefits of marriage for any two or more people who claim to have homosexual tendencies.

It is a perfect storm.

These radical objectives, which seemed

unthinkable just a few years ago, have largely been achieved or are now within reach. All that remains is for the movement and its friends to deliver the coup de grâce to a beleaguered institution that has held society together since earliest recorded history. Those of us in North America and Europe are not simply "slouching towards Gomorrah," as Judge Robert Bork warned in his bestselling book[7]; we are hurtling toward it.

To cite another metaphor, the old earthen dam that has held and protected the reservoir of Judeo-Christian values and beliefs since the days of our Founding Fathers has been leaking for decades. With each passing year, the structural damage has become greater. But in recent days, the entire superstructure appears to have given way.

Thousands of homosexuals in a handful of cities have procured official marriage licenses, representing the collapse of the rule of law. These blatant illegalities have encountered only sporadic opposition from legal and governmental officials. And there are more outrageous developments to come.

A revolution of striking proportions now looms before us. As you will see in subsequent chapters, the movement has become a tsunami—a tidal wave that threatens to overwhelm anyone who stands in its way. I do not recall a time when the institution of marriage faced such danger, or when the forces arrayed against it were more formidable or determined. Barring a miracle, the family as it has been known from time immemorial will crumble. This is a moment for greater courage and wisdom than we have ever been called upon to exercise.

In a recent *National Review Online* article, Maggie Gallagher wrote, "Gay marriage is not some sideline issue, it *is* the marriage debate." She noted, "The consequences of our current retreat from marriage is not a flourishing libertarian social order, but a gigantic expansion of state power and a vast increase in social disorder and human suffering."[8]

Gallagher's dire warning was echoed in a *Boston Globe* editorial by Jeff Jacoby. He noted, "The adoption of same-sex marriage would topple a long-standing system of shared values. It would change assumptions and expectations by which society has long operated—that men and women are not interchangeable, for example, and that the central reason for marriage is to provide children with mothers and fathers in a safe and loving environment."[9]

Jacoby continued, "My foreboding is that a generation after same-sex marriage is legalized, families will be even less stable than they are today, the divorce rate will be even higher and children will be even less safe. To express such a dire warning is to be labeled an alarmist, a reactionary, a bigot and worse.... But it is not bigotry to try to learn from history, or to point out that some institutions have stood the test of time because they are the only ones that *can* stand the test of time."[10]

AWAKENING TO THE DANGER

But now let me give you some very good news. I am encouraged and strengthened by undeniable evidences that the institutional church is awakening at last. For nearly thirty years, I have been hoping and praying that pastors and their Bible-believing congregations would recognize the dangers that have been directed toward everything they have stood for. I remember sitting in church in the 1970s and praying that Christian leaders would respond to the arguments of the Sexual Revolution and the attack on morality posed by the likes of Hugh Hefner and

Phil Donahue. Some pastors rose to the challenge, but many did not. Too often there was silence on our end of the line.

At last, however, something dramatic is happening on that front. Just as the attack on Pearl Harbor in 1941 by the empire of Japan served to energize and mobilize the armed forces of the United States, it would appear that the vicious assault on marriage and the church in recent months has begun to reinvigorate people of faith. I see indications that the church is marshaling its forces and preparing to meet the challenge. Evil has a way of overreaching, and that appears to have happened regarding the blatant and lawless assault on marriage and biblical morality. In a strange way, the threats we are facing today could be the vehicle for a revitalized church. It is an exciting thing to watch.

As a case in point, I was asked to speak in May 2004 at a rally in Seattle, which was organized by Dr. Ken Hutcherson and his fellow pastors in the area. It was called "Mayday for Marriage" and was held at Safeco Field, where baseball's Mariners play. Though the pastors only had thirty days to organize the rally, there were more than twenty thousand highly engaged participants on hand that day.[11]

About three hundred homosexual protestors were also in the stands, where they yelled and screamed for two hours. At one point early in my speech, I stopped and turned to the detractors. I said, "I want you to know that we welcome you here. You have every right to fight for what you believe, and we are glad you came. But we disagree with your agenda for the family, and we will do what we can to defend it." With that, twenty thousand people stood with their arms outstretched toward the protestors and cheered for them with a deafening roar.

A few weeks earlier, I was invited to speak to pastors in the Portland, Oregon, area. We expected a thousand members of the clergy to be in attendance, but there were twenty-two hundred on hand from all over the state. This is the largest such assembly of clergy members ever held in that city. Their participation on a Monday, typically a pastor's day off, is a testament to the concern evidenced there. The night before the event, I met Dr. Frank Damazio, Tim Nashif, and the other organizers at City Bible Church. After getting acquainted, they asked if I would like to go downstairs where a prayer meeting was being held for the preservation of marriage and for the activities of the next day. I expected to see twenty or thirty people gathered to pray, but instead I found one thousand people standing and praying out loud with their hands in the air. I could not contain my emotion. Obviously, something dramatic is taking place in the Pacific Northwest, where the threat to the family is being met by a determined faith community.

It is happening elsewhere, too. Similar rallies have already occurred in San Francisco, Chicago, San Jose, and Atlanta.[12] An event scheduled to be held in Washington DC in October 2004 is expected to draw one million couples.

There is more good news on the horizon. The United Methodist Church, after three years of bitter debate and wrangling, decided on May 4, 2004, to reaffirm both their opposition to homosexuality and their ban on ordaining non-celibate homosexuals.[13]

They are not alone. For more than thirty years, the Presbyterian Church (USA) has been successfully resisting the relentless charge of a minority who desire the acceptance of homosexual clergy and even gay marriage itself.[14] I applaud their steadfast and tireless stance. Likewise, the Southern Baptists have stood strong in the face of a media campaign that's committed to mischaracterizing their opposition to homosexuality as bigotry. These and other denominations deserve our commendation for resisting the powerful forces that have attempted to "reform" the church and its theology. We must remain ever vigilant, for in the words of Margaret Thatcher, the former prime minister of England, "now is not the time to go wobbly."[15]

Not only is the church beginning to address this issue, but state legislatures are swinging into action, too. As of this writing, thirty-eight states have passed "Defense of Marriage Acts," or DOMAs.[16] Although the courts could override them, these legislative maneuvers make it clear that families are important and elected officials recognize their responsibility to defend them. Meanwhile, nearly a dozen states are considering constitutional amendments to protect marriage.[17] Clearly, the majority of citizens in this country are not going to let the family collapse without a fight.

There is hope. We can still turn the tide. Most Americans want marriage to survive. But we need a widespread awakening that will shake the nation, and we need it soon.

Isn't it worth our utmost efforts to protect the

health and vitality of the traditional family? On that one institution rests the welfare of future generations and the viability of this great land. Indeed, Western civilization itself appears to hang in the balance. We must not throw this God-ordained institution on the ash heap of history.

2

HOW DID WE GET IN THIS MESS?

When Nazi Germany marched its troops into Austria and then "annexed" Czechoslovakia in the late 1930s—signaling Adolf Hitler's dangerous and frightening intentions—the response from the rest of Europe was startling: It did nothing. France quaked in its boots. Russia tried to cut a deal. The Swiss and the Swedes declared themselves neutral. The Italians joined forces with Germany. And England's Prime Minister Neville Chamberlain and his political allies staked their hopes on a policy of appeasement. Essentially their strategy was to ignore the threat, give Hitler what he wanted, and hope against hope that the trouble would soon pass. It didn't.

Hitler continued his grab for power and eventually subjugated most of the people of Europe to tyranny and slavery. Chamberlain was forced to resign in shame. Before long, Britain stood alone against the Fascist forces. Only the courage and faith of the British people—rallied by their determined new prime minister, Winston Churchill—enabled them to withstand the onslaught of the Nazi blitzkrieg and, with the help of the United States and the Allied forces, gradually turn the tide of war. The crisis was resolved, but only barely; and the cost was staggering. Millions of men, women, and children lost their lives in the battle for freedom. Churchill called it the most preventable conflict in history, saying, "Never was a war more easy to stop than that which has just wrecked what was left of the world from the previous struggle."[18] Cowardice and timidity had ruled the day. Europe's apathetic response to Germany's goose-stepping militarism allowed a ruthless dictator to bring the world to the brink of a long, dark night of oppression.

Today, more than six decades later and on the other side of the Atlantic Ocean, we find ourselves in a terrible battle of a different sort, but one that also threatens the very existence of our society. This struggle is not being fought with guns and bombs, but with ideas, with creative uses of the law, and with methods of intimidation. It is a battle for the very soul of the nation.

Prior to the recent stirrings within the church, America's response to the threat has been a shameful echo of Neville Chamberlain's pusillanimous and pathetic reply. "Maybe," many of my countrymen seem to feel, "if we ignore those who oppose us, it will just go away." This is precisely what the majority of our political leaders are still saying about the issue. There are, as I write, less than one-third of the United States Senate standing up for marriage.[19] According to senatorial sources, only ten senators are willing to actively speak up on the issue. What a tragedy. The future of the nation is in crisis, yet the appeasers appear to be thinking only of themselves and their political fiefdoms. Those who will not speak up in this time of great moral crisis don't deserve to hold the offices to which we have elected them.

Why should we be surprised by the lack of commitment to the family in contemporary Washington? That has been the case for many years.

Congress, in its consuming self-interest, has never cared much about the family. For thirty-two years, Democrats and Republicans foolishly taxed traditional marriages at a higher rate than those who irresponsibly cohabited.[20] At long last, the Bush Administration addressed our concerns in 2001, and congress is expected to make the tax cut permanent.

President Bill Clinton stood on the White House lawn near the end of his second term and told members of the press that to let families keep more of their own money would effectively "squander" the surplus.[21] Was that outrageous or what? The president, speaking on behalf of a government that squanders untold millions of dollars every day, was worried about moms and dads wasting their own money—money that he thought should have been sent to Washington for safekeeping. Though I searched for a reply from the media, I could not find a peep of protest from those who are supposed to protect the public interest.

So the "marriage penalty" tax survived through the nineties. Mothers and fathers who were taking care of children, packing lunches, helping with homework, tucking kids into bed at night, and saying prayers over them carried a greater tax burden than those who simply lived together out of wedlock. Our representatives knew of that inequity, yet they steadfastly refused to address it until goaded by the Bush Administration. Congress's disregard for the family revealed its lack of appreciation for the vital role this historic institution has played in maintaining the health and strength of the nation. Meanwhile, the vitality of families continued to decline.

In 1999, sociologists Dr. Barbara Dafoe Whitehead and Dr. David Popenoe, both from Rutgers University, released the results of a longitudinal study that confirmed the trends: The family as we have known it is passing from the scene.[22] The study should have made headlines across the country, prompting legislators to address the need. But the nation yawned.

In 2001, when the U.S. Census Bureau released its report from the previous decade, the results confirmed the conclusions from Whitehead and Popenoe. The data revealed again that the traditional family is dying. Households headed by single fathers had increased in that ten years by 72 percent; households headed by single mothers had increased by 25 percent; and households headed by traditional married couples had dropped below 25 percent for the first time in history. Thirty-three percent of all babies were born to unmarried women, compared to only 3.8 percent in 1940.[23] Those of us who have worked to defend the family were shocked by the rapid deterioration of this great institution. Still, official Washington was, and is, unperturbed.

To our political leaders, it was as though the problems on the home front didn't exist. Margaret LaMontaine, the White House Domestic Policy Advisor to President George W. Bush, was interviewed on C-Span shortly after the release of the census report. Asked for her reaction to the findings, she said, "So what?"[24] She apparently saw no cause for concern. Fortunately, she didn't speak for the president in that regard. The Bush Administration has since asked Congress for $360 million per year to shore up the institution of marriage with counseling and training programs,[25] but Democrats and a few liberal Republicans in Congress fought tooth and nail to defeat the initiative. These political leaders who have spent trillions of our tax dollars, often on expenditures designed to help them get reelected, clearly resent and oppose any program that might help rescue the beleaguered family. The institution of marriage obviously has very few friends in the nation's capital. Again, why are we shocked when the reaction to the present attack on the family is little more than a yawn? It is par for the course.

Do I sound frustrated over this lack of commitment to the welfare of the family? You bet I do, because our leaders in Washington appear fully prepared to let it fail. I have been meeting with lawmakers on Capitol Hill about family issues for more than twenty years and have never had one of them refuse to see me. That is, until this issue of homosexual marriage came on the scene. During a recent visit to Washington, several pro-family leaders and I attempted to meet with eleven Democratic senators about the defense of marriage. Not one of them would see us. We were flatly turned down by Senators Evan Bayh (IN), Jeff Bingaman (NM), Robert Byrd (WV), Bob Graham (FL), Ernest Hollings (SC), Bill Nelson (FL), Mark Pryor (AR), John Breaux (LA), Mary Landrieu (LA), Ben Nelson (NE), and Blanche Lincoln (AR). These and other politicians are scared to death of this issue and do not want to be seen consorting with conservative Christians. They need to hear from their constituents, both in their local offices and in the Senate.

Not till they feel the heat will they see the light.

Senator Orrin Hatch (R-UT) and Senator Jim Talent (R-MO), both of whom I consider to be personal friends, called me to discuss the Federal Marriage Amendment, but they had a better idea to suggest. Instead of a constitutional amendment to protect marriage, they were considering sending a proposal to Congress that would leave the matter to the states to decide. These men are experienced and knowledgeable enough to know that this is a first-class cop-out. Many of their colleagues have begun feeding their constituents the same unworkable idea. To let the states define what is and is not a marriage will mean fifty different definitions. That would create utter chaos. Can you imagine a couple being legally married in Texas and not married in Connecticut? Furthermore, the Supreme Court will override whatever the states do anyway, just as it did with regard to abortion in 1973. We must have a constitutional amendment to protect the family. There is no other answer.

We must remember that behind the public policy debates and media influences are real human beings who are affected adversely by the disintegration of families. Among them are millions of hurting people—husbands, wives, and children—for whom everything stable and predictable has been shattered. They represent the agonies of loving wives who committed themselves wholly and unreservedly to men who later rejected them for other lovers. There are husbands who are struggling to raise their kids alone because their wives decided they didn't want to be mothers anymore. And, of course, the breakup of families results in millions of pitiful children who cry themselves to sleep at night because they miss their mom or their dad who is not there to give them a hug or make them a treat. This is the legacy of divorce and sexual promiscuity. Social experimentation has produced these tiny victims who cry out for compassion and understanding. It is why I have committed my life to their cause and will continue to do so for as long as God gives me the strength.

A RECENT HISTORY OF REDEFINING MARRIAGE

To understand more about how marriage came to be so fragile after it had survived for so long, we have to take a stroll through recent history. One of the earliest and most damaging blows came in 1969, when the world's first no-fault divorce law, developed by radical family-law theorists, was signed into law in California.[26] With the stroke of a pen, "till death do us part" became optional. Suddenly, it was easier for a spouse to legally get out of a thirty-year marriage than it was to break a pool maintenance contract!

In the years that followed, every state adopted some form of no-fault divorce, and for the first time in our nation's history, the understanding of marriage as a permanent social and spiritual contract was no longer backed by law. And once heterosexuals dismissed the essential "as long as we both shall live" component of marriage, it was only a matter of time before someone tried to do away with the fundamental "husband and wife" part.

The growth and normalization of cohabitation—which our parents and past generations of parents referred to as "living in sin"—has also had a devastating impact. It has increased 850 percent since 1960.[27] Add to this a third failed social experiment—the Sexual Revolution and its consequent rise in out-of-wedlock births—and you can see how marriage and children have suffered. "Make love, not war!" shouted the sixties' students and flower children, who not only proceeded to make millions of unwanted babies, but demanded the right to kill them in the womb. The family was rocked to its foundation. And in the process, sexually transmitted diseases reached epidemic proportions, including the onset of the HIV/AIDS epidemic.

The result of these departures from the Judeo-Christian system of values has been the destabilization of marriage and the introduction of other "new" ideas now being floated by the media. Today, those who helped to tear down the historic family are using the weaknesses they helped to create as justification for homosexual marriage. "It couldn't be worse than what we've got" has been the retort.

And now the nation's courts have wreaked havoc on the institution of marriage. In one decision after another, the judiciary has torn into the fabric of the home. I won't review all those unfortunate cases at this point, but there is one that stands above the rest. On June 26, 2003, the U.S. Supreme Court considered the legality of homosexual behavior and found that, lo and behold, the Constitution guaranteed a right to sodomy.[28] Yep, it was tucked right there (somewhere) in the original document.

With this ruling, our Founding Fathers must have rolled in their graves. Our august justices "made up" this new constitutional right and used it to strike down the Texas law prohibiting sodomy. The case is now known as the infamous *Lawrence v. Texas* decision.[29] Very few Americans agreed with the decision, but they were never asked. They no longer determine their own destinies. Abraham Lincoln said in the Gettysburg Address that ours is a government "of the people, by the people, and for the people," and yet "the people" have now been co-opted by an unelected and unaccountable judiciary, appointed for life, that determines all the great moral issues of our day. Each time the Supremes meet, it's as though they are holding a "Constitutional Convention," because the foundational document becomes whatever any five of these justices say it is. This is called an *oligarchy*—a government by the few—and it is taking us ever further down the road to moral relativism.

Writing for the majority in the Lawrence case, Justice Anthony Kennedy—whom I consider to be the most dangerous man in America because of his determination to rewrite the Constitution—stated that, speaking of the prohibition of sodomy, the law's "continuance as precedent demeans the lives of homosexual persons."[30] By ruling that sodomy is a constitutionally protected "right," the highest court in the land declared, in effect, that considerations of morality and decency were irrelevant.

It was this regrettable decision that has created the present turmoil throughout the nation. It has emboldened rogue commissioners, mayors, and legislators to begin overriding laws prohibiting homosexual marriage. They have been passing out marriage licenses like candy. These minor bureaucrats now have things going their way, and they are going to strike while the iron is hot. This is why we are in the state of peril that faces our nation today. Like Adolf Hitler, who overran his European neighbors, those who favor homosexual marriage are determined to make it legal, regardless of the democratic processes that stand in their way.

The Massachusetts Supreme Judicial Court was the first authority of its stature to grab the opportunity provided by Lawrence. It ruled 4 to 3 in November 2003 that the state legislature had to recognize the legitimacy of homosexual "marriage."[31]

Since when, we would ask, has one branch of government had the power to order another to do its bidding? Whatever happened to the principle of checks and balances, wherein governmental agencies of equivalent status served to limit the power of the others? Clearly, the Massachusetts Supreme Judicial Court considers its power to be preeminent. But who gave them that authority? Certainly not the people of Massachusetts.

On May 17, perhaps the worst day for the institution of marriage in the history of the world, Massachusetts began issuing licenses to homosexuals.[32] Most of those couples are now legally married and are fanning out across the nation, demanding recognition of their new legal status. It will be very difficult to reverse course. Furthermore, even if a pending state constitutional amendment is ratified by the people, "civil unions" will be legalized, making them the equivalent of marriage-in-everything-but-name.[33] Marriage is, indeed, under fire in nations around the world.

As of this writing, lawless local officials have issued marriage licenses to homosexual couples in defiance of state laws in California, Oregon, New Mexico, New York, and New Jersey.[34] Behind them all is the Lawrence decision and the implications of the ruling, making it clear that the Supreme Court intends to "find" within the Constitution a right for homosexuals to marry. All that is hindering that momentous decision is an appropriate case that finds its way up to the Supreme Court. That is why the Constitution must be amended to checkmate the imperious Court.

There is only one way to get the attention of our leaders in Washington, who have the power to change the makeup of the court and to pass protective legislation. We need to overwhelm them with calls, e-mails, visits, letters, and publications, and most importantly, we need to support their opponents. That gets their attention because, for most of our representatives in Congress, what they care largely about is staying in power. When their coveted positions are threatened, they tend to do what is right. In the meantime, the responsibility to preserve marriage rests with those of us who recognize the gravity of the situation. This is no time for appeasement.

Meanwhile, the institution of marriage hobbles along, struggling to survive the assaults being made on it. We must give it a helping hand.

3

WHY WE MUST WIN THIS BATTLE

An argument in favor of homosexual marriage that you are likely to hear again and again on radio talk shows, national television, and the Internet reflects a line of reasoning that you must be prepared to counter. It is embodied in these kinds of questions: Why all the fuss about gay marriage, anyway? And why should it matter to you if a gay couple marries and moves into your neighborhood? Why shouldn't our definition of family be broadened and modernized? After all, what harm could possibly be done by yielding to the demands of those who say traditional notions of family are outmoded and irrelevant?

Columnist Steve Blow, in a recent edition of the *Dallas Morning News,* echoed some of these questions. His op-ed piece was titled "Gay Marriage: Why Would It Affect Me?" and was apparently written after he had read one of my recent newsletters on the subject. Blow wrote:

> When opponents talk about the "defense of marriage," they lose me. James Dobson's Focus on the Family just sent out a mailer to 2.5 million homes saying: "The homosexual activists' movement is poised to administer a devastating and potentially fatal blow to the traditional family." And I say, "Huh?" How does anyone's pledge of love and commitment turn into a fatal blow to families?[35]

Mr. Blow clearly believes that the only reason for not legalizing homosexual marriage is sheer bigotry. Nothing could be further from the truth. There are very compelling arguments against marriage between homosexuals that should be considered by anyone who has not yet become familiar with the issues. Unfortunately, the American people as a whole have not yet thought through the consequences and measured the impact of this revolutionary concept. I could list fifty or more legitimate concerns. Let me focus on eleven.

1. The legalization of homosexual marriage will quickly destroy the traditional family.

We've already seen evidence from the Scandinavian countries that de facto homosexual marriage destroys the real McCoy. These two entities cannot coexist because they represent opposite ends of the universe. A book could be written on the reasons for this collision between matter and antimatter, but I will cite three of them.

First, when the state sanctions homosexual relationships and gives them its blessing, the younger generation becomes confused about sexual identity and quickly loses its understanding of lifelong commitments, emotional bonding, sexual purity, the role of children in a family, and, from a spiritual perspective, the "sanctity" of marriage. Marriage is reduced to something of a partnership that provides attractive benefits and sexual convenience but cannot offer the intimacy described in Genesis. Cohabitation and short-term relationships are the inevitable result. Ask the Norwegians, the Swedes, and the people from the Netherlands. That is exactly what is happening there.[36]

Second, the introduction of legalized gay marriages will lead inexorably to polygamy and other alternatives to one-man/one-woman unions. In Utah, polygamist Tom Green, who claims five wives, is citing *Lawrence v. Texas* as the legal authority for his appeal.[37] In January 2004, a Salt Lake City civil rights attorney filed a federal lawsuit on behalf of another couple wanting to engage in legal polygamy.[38] Their justification? *Lawrence v. Texas.* The ACLU of Utah has actually suggested that the state will "have to step up to prove that a polygamous relationship is detrimental to society"—as opposed to the polygamists having to prove that plural marriage is not harmful to the culture.[39] Do you see how the game is played? The responsibility to defend the family now rests on you and me to prove that polygamy is unhealthy. The ACLU went on to say that the nuclear family "may not be necessarily the best model."[40] Indeed, Justice Antonin Scalia warned of this likelihood in his statement for the minority in the Lawrence case.[41] It took less than six months for his prediction to become a reality.

Why will gay marriage set the table for polygamy? Because there is no place to stop once that Rubicon has been crossed. Historically, the definition of marriage has rested on a foundation of tradition, legal precedent, theology, and the overwhelming support of the people. After the introduction of marriage between homosexuals, however, it will be supported by nothing more substantial than the opinion of a single judge or by a black-robed panel of justices. After they have reached their dubious decisions, the family will consist of little more than someone's interpretation of "rights." Given that unstable legal climate, it is certain that some self-possessed judge, somewhere, will soon rule that three men or three women can marry. Or five men and two women. Or four and four. Who will be able to deny them that right? The guarantee is implied, we will be told, by the Constitution. Those who disagree will continue to be seen as hatemongers and bigots. (Indeed, those charges are already being leveled against Christians who espouse biblical values!) How about group marriage? Or marriage between daddies and little girls? How about marriage between a man and his donkey? Anything allegedly linked to "civil rights" will be doable. The legal underpinnings for marriage will have been destroyed.

The third reason marriage between homosexuals will destroy traditional marriage is that this is the ultimate goal of activists, and they will not stop until they achieve it. The history of the gay and lesbian movement has been that its adherents quickly move the goal line as soon as the previous one has been breached, revealing even more shocking and outrageous objectives. In the present instance, homosexual activists, heady with power and exhilaration, feel the political climate is right to tell us what they have wanted all along. This is the real deal: Most gays and lesbians do *not* want to marry each other. That would entangle them in all sorts of legal constraints. Who needs a lifetime commitment to one person? *The intention here is to create an entirely different legal structure.*

With marriage as we know it gone, everyone would enjoy all the legal benefits of marriage (custody rights, tax-free inheritance, joint ownership of property, health care and spousal citizenship, etc.) without limiting the number of partners or their gender. Nor would "couples" be bound to each other in the eyes of the law. This is clearly where the movement is headed. If you doubt that this is the motive, read what is in the literature today. Activists have created a new word to replace the outmoded terms *infidelity*, *adultery*, *cheating*, and *promiscuity*. The new concept is *polyamorous*. It means the same thing (literally "many loves") but with the agreement of the primary sexual partner. Why not? He or she is probably polyamorous, too.

Liberal columnist Michael Kinsley wrote a July 2003 op-ed piece in the *Washington Post* titled "Abolish Marriage: Let's Really Get the Government Out of Our Bedrooms."[42] In this revealing editorial, Kinsley writes:

> [The] solution is to end the institution of marriage, or rather, the solution is to end the institution of government monopoly on marriage. And yes, if three people want to get married, or one person wants to marry herself and someone else wants to conduct a ceremony and declare them married, let 'em. If you and your government aren't implicated, what do you care? If marriage were an entirely private affair, all the disputes over gay marriages would become irrelevant.

Otherwise, the author warns, "it's going to get ugly."[43]

Judith Levine, writing in the *Village Voice*, offered support for these ideas in an article titled "Stop the Wedding: Why Gay Marriage Isn't Radical Enough."[44] She wrote, "Because American marriage is inextricable from Christianity, it admits participants as Noah let animals on the ark. But it doesn't have to be that way. In 1972 the National Coalition of Gay Organizations demanded the 'repeal of all legislative provisions that restrict the sex or number of persons entering into a marriage unit; and the extension of legal benefits to all persons who cohabit regardless of sex or numbers.' Group marriage could comprise any combination of genders."[45]

Stanley Kurtz, a research fellow at the Hoover Institution, summed up the situation in a recent *Weekly Standard* article. He noted that if gay marriage is legalized, "marriage will be transformed into a variety of relationship contracts, linking two, three or more individuals (however weakly or temporarily) in every conceivable combination of male and female...the bottom of this slope is visible from where we now stand."[46]

We must all become soberly aware of a deeply disturbing reality: The homosexual agenda is *not* marriage for gays. It is marriage for no one. And despite what you read or see in the media, it is definitely *not* monogamous.

What will happen sociologically if marriage becomes anything or everything or nothing? The short answer is that the state will lose its compelling interest in marital relationships altogether. After marriage has been redefined, divorces will be obtained instantly, will not involve a court, and will take on the status of a driver's license or a hunting permit. With the family out of the way, all rights and privileges of marriage will accrue to gay and lesbian partners without the legal entanglements and commitments heretofore associated with it.

These are just a few reasons why homosexual marriage is truly revolutionary. Legalizing it will change everything, especially for the institution of the family.

2. Children will suffer most.

The implications for children in a world of decaying families are profound. Because homosexuals are rarely monogamous, often having as many as three hundred[47] or more partners in a lifetime—some studies say it is typically more than one thousand[48]—children in those polyamorous situations are caught in a perpetual coming and going. It is devastating to kids, who by their nature are enormously conservative creatures. They like things to stay just the way they are, and they hate change. Some have been known to eat the same brand of peanut butter throughout childhood.

More than ten thousand studies have concluded that kids do best when they are raised by loving and committed mothers and fathers.[49] They are less likely to be on illegal drugs, less likely to be retained in a grade, less likely to drop out of school, less likely to commit suicide, less likely to be in poverty, less likely to become juvenile delinquents, and, for the girls, less likely to become teen mothers. They are healthier both emotionally and physically, even thirty years later, than those not so blessed with traditional parents.[50]

Social scientists have been surprisingly consistent in warning about the impact of fractured families. If present trends continue, the majority of children will have several "moms" and "dads," perhaps six or eight "grandparents," and dozens of half-siblings. It will be a world where little boys and girls are shuffled from pillar to post in an ever-changing pattern of living arrangements; where huge numbers of them will be raised in foster homes or living on the street, as millions do in countries all over the world today. Imagine an environment where nothing is stable and where people think primarily about themselves and their own self-preservation. And have you considered what will happen when homosexuals with children become divorced? Instead of two moms and two dads, they will have to contend with four moms or four dads. How would you like to be a new husband a generation later who instantly had four or six or eight mothers-in-law?

We must also consider a world of the future where immorality is even more rampant than today, where both unbridled homosexual *and* heterosexual liaisons are the norm. The apostle Paul described such a society in the book of Romans, referring apparently to ancient Rome: "They have become filled with every kind of wickedness, evil, greed and depravity. They are full of envy, murder, strife, deceit and malice. They are gossips, slanderers, God-haters, insolent, arrogant and boastful; they invent ways of doing evil; they disobey their parents; they are senseless, faithless, heartless, ruthless" (1:29–31).

It appears likely now that the demise of families will accelerate this type of decline dramatically, resulting in a chaotic culture that will rip kids apart emotionally.

3. Public schools in every state will embrace homosexuality.

With the legalization of homosexual marriage, every public school in the nation will be required to teach this perversion as the moral equivalent of traditional marriage between a man and a woman. Textbooks, even in conservative regions, will have to depict man/man and woman/woman relationships, and stories written for children as young as elementary school, or even kindergarten, will have to give equal space and emphasis to homosexuals. How can a child, fresh out of toddlerhood, comprehend the meaning of adult sexuality? The answer is that they can't—yet it is happening in the state of California already.[51]

4. Adoption laws will be instantly obsolete.

From the moment homosexual marriage becomes legal, courts will not be able to favor a traditional coupling of one man and one woman in matters of adoption. Children will be placed in homes with parents representing only one sex on an equal basis with those having a mom and a dad. Even the polyamorous couples won't be excluded. The prospect of fatherless and motherless children will not be considered in the evaluation of eligibility. It will be the law.

5. Foster-care programs will be impacted dramatically.

Foster-care parents will be required to undergo "sensitivity training" to rid themselves of bias in favor of heterosexuality, and will have to affirm homosexuality in children and teens. Moral training, at least as it applies to sexuality, will be forbidden. Again, this is the current law in California.[52]

6. The health care system will stagger and perhaps collapse.

This could be the straw that breaks the back of the insurance industry in Western nations, as millions of new dependents become eligible for coverage. Every HIV-positive patient needs only to find a partner to receive the same coverage as offered to an employee. It is estimated by some analysts that drastic increases in premiums can be anticipated and that it may not be profitable for companies to stay in business.

And how about the cost to American businesses? Will they be able to provide health benefits? If not, can physicians, nurses, and technicians be expected to work for nothing or to provide their services in exchange for a vague promise of payments from indigent patients? Try selling that to a neurosurgeon or an orthopedist who has to pay increased premiums for malpractice insurance. The entire health care system could implode.

7. Social Security will be severely stressed.

Again, with millions of new eligible dependents, what will happen to the Social Security system, which is already facing bankruptcy? If it does collapse, what will that mean for elderly people who must rely totally on that meager support? Who is thinking through these draconian possibilities as we careen toward "a brave new world"?

8. Religious freedom will almost certainly be jeopardized.

In order to get a perspective on where the homosexual activist movement is taking us, one can simply look at our neighbors to the north. Canada is leading the way on this revolutionary path. I could cite dozens of examples indicating that religious freedom in that country is dying. Indeed, on April 28, 2004, the Parliament passed Bill C-250, which effectively criminalized speech or writings that criticize homosexuality.[53] Anything deemed to be "homophobic" is punishable by six months in prison or other severe penalties.[54]

Pastors and priests in Canada are wondering if they can preach from Leviticus or Romans 1 or other passages from the writings of the apostle Paul. Will a new Bible be mandated that is bereft of "hate speech"? Consider this: A man who owned a printing press in Canada was fined over $40,000 for refusing to print stationery for a homosexual activist organization.[55]

Censorship is already in full swing. One of our Focus on the Family radio programs on the subject of homosexuality was judged by the Canadian Radio and Television Commission to be "homophobic." The radio station that carried the broadcast was censured for airing it, and I have not been able to address the issue in Canada since.

Is that kind of censorship coming to the United States? Yes, I believe it is. Once homosexual marriage is legalized nationwide, if indeed that is where we are headed, laws based on "equality" will bring many changes in the law. Furthermore, it is likely that nonprofit organizations that refuse to hire homosexuals on religious grounds will lose their tax exemptions. Some Christian colleges and universities are already worrying about that possibility.

9. Other nations are watching our march toward homosexual marriage and will follow our lead.

Marriage among homosexuals will spread throughout the world, just as pornography did after the Nixon Commission declared obscene material "beneficial" to mankind.[56] Almost instantly, the English-speaking countries liberalized their laws against smut. America continues to be the fountainhead of filth and immorality, and its influence is global. Dr. Darrell Reid, president of Focus on the Family Canada, told me recently that his country is carefully monitoring what is happening in the United States. If we take this step off a cliff, the family on every continent will splinter at an accelerated rate. Conversely, our Supreme Court has made it clear that it looks to European and Canadian law in the interpretation of our Constitution.[57] What an outrage! That should have been grounds for impeachment, but Congress, as usual, remained passive and silent.

10. The gospel of Jesus Christ will be severely curtailed.

The family has been God's primary vehicle for evangelism since the beginning. Its most important assignment has been the propagation of the human race and the handing down of the faith to our children. Malachi 2:15, which refers to husbands and wives, reads, "Has not the LORD made them one? In flesh and spirit they are his. And why one? Because he was seeking godly offspring. So guard yourself in your spirit, and do not break faith with the wife of your youth." That responsibility to teach the next generation will never recover from the loss of committed, God-fearing families. The younger generation and those yet to come will be deprived of the Good News, as has already occurred in France, Germany, and other European countries. Instead of providing for a father and mother, the advent of homosexual marriage will create millions of motherless and fatherless kids. Are we now going to join the Netherlands and Belgium to become the third country in the history of the world to "normalize" and legalize behavior that has been prohibited by God Himself? Heaven help us if we do!

11. The culture war will be over, and the world may soon become "as it was in the days of Noah" (Matthew 24:37).

This is the climactic moment in the battle to preserve the family, and future generations hang in the balance. This apocalyptic and pessimistic view of the institution of the family and its future will sound alarmist to many, but I think it will prove accurate unless—*unless*—God's people awaken and begin an even greater vigil of prayer for our nation. That's why we are urgently seeking the Lord's favor and asking Him to hear the petitions of His people and heal our land. Despite some of the positive developments mentioned earlier, large segments of the church still appear to be unaware of the danger; church leaders are surprisingly silent about our peril (although we are tremendously thankful for the efforts of those who have spoken out on this issue).

This reticence on behalf of Christians is deeply troubling. Marriage is a sacrament designed by God that serves as a metaphor for the relationship between Christ and His church. Tampering with His plan for the family is immoral and wrong. To violate the

Lord's expressed will for humankind, especially in regard to behavior that He has prohibited, is to court disaster.

4

SPEAKING THE TRUTH IN LOVE

Americans know intuitively that something is wrong with the idea of legally endorsing same-sex "marriages." We see this discomfort in public opinion polls: Two-thirds of Americans are opposed to "gay marriage."[58] On the other hand, many of our countrymen are reluctant to talk about the issues because, as columnist Kathleen Parker put it, most of us know and/or love someone who is gay and don't want to deny them respect and happiness. So "we sit back quietly and watch the reordering of society for fear of hurting a loved one's feelings or offending a coworker."[59]

I understand Parker's point and have, in the past, been reluctant to address the issue for the same reason. However, considering the level of aggression coming from today's homosexual activist community, our back is to the wall. Homosexual activists are determined to ignore existing laws that protect the institution of marriage and to co-opt the family for their own purposes. They have left us but two choices: Either meekly acquiesce to a wide range of revolutionary cultural demands, or stand up and fight for the things we believe in. I have chosen the second option, and I pray that millions of other Americans will respectfully do the same.

THE INTIMIDATION FACTOR

Homosexual activists know that most Christians are uncomfortable in today's highly charged political arena. We are, for the most part, peace-loving people who do not like angry confrontation and bitter debate. Our philosophical opponents understand this, which explains why they often react with in-your-face rhetoric and behavior. Their purpose is to intimidate those who oppose their agenda.

One of their most effective tactics is to depict Christians—and others who uphold traditional values—as "hateful," calling us "bigots" and the dreaded (and nonsensical) "homophobe." No one wants to be called names, and the intimidation factor keeps many from speaking out on this topic. The shouting and blustering of homosexual activists is not unlike that of a rebellious teen who slams doors, throws things around, and threatens to run away. Most parents have had to deal with this kind of behavior and have learned that giving in at such a time can be disastrous for both parties. What's needed is loving firmness in the face of temper tantrums and accusations.

Another common tactic of activists today is to hurl the charge of "homophobia" at anyone who disagrees with the movement in the slightest detail. Everything we contend is called "hate speech" or "gay bashing." Christians are very vulnerable to these accusations, because hate is the antithesis of what Jesus taught. It cuts us to the quick to be charged with hypocrisy for departing from the tenets of the faith. But before we accept the name-calling as valid, we should recognize that in many instances those who hurl accusations at us don't even *believe* the charges—they are merely ruses conjured by the movement to silence those with the courage to speak. How do I know these are trumped-up accusations? Because I have been victimized by them.

In 1998, when a young homosexual named Matthew Shepard was murdered by two thugs in Wyoming, the media immediately accused some of us in the pro-family movement of creating a hateful environment that encouraged this kind of violence.[60] It was a ridiculous claim, but I got tagged along with several colleagues. Katie Couric of NBC's *Today Show* asked a guest one morning if he thought the leaders of Focus on the Family, the Christian Coalition, and the Family Research Council were indirectly responsible for Shepard's murder because of the venom we espoused.[61] This was an outrageous suggestion that, frankly, I resented. There is no evidence that the killers had ever heard of me, read any of my books, or visited our campus. In twenty-seven years I have never said anything hateful about homosexuals on our broadcast, and I do not condone violence or disrespect for anyone. Yet, in asking the question, sweet little Katie planted the notion that Christians are somehow responsible for the hatred that allegedly stalks our land.

Of course, Couric cited no evidence to validate her question, because there isn't any. Every word I have publicly spoken in more than two decades, as well as everything I have written, is on record. You would think that Couric would feel obligated to come up with a single hateful phrase or idea we've put forward that has been hurtful to homosexuals. She didn't. She simply impugned the reputations of conservatives who were innocent of wrongdoing.

This kind of Christian bashing has become routine in the secular media. Why? Because the personal attacks on us are part of a liberal strategy to silence the opposition. For instance, Hillary Clinton blamed the "vast right-wing conspiracy" when her husband was accused of sexual misconduct with an intern.[62] The president later admitted he lied to the country about Monica Lewinsky, but the first lady never apologized.[63]

New York Times columnist Frank Rich is a member of the media who routinely bashes Christians. Immediately after the Oklahoma City bombing in 1995, Rich speculated that the bombers were probably right-wing Christians.[64] He did not—nor could he—support such speculation. After Timothy McVeigh and Terry Nichols were tried and convicted of the crime, I wrote to Rich and asked him to admit that he had falsely accused Christians. He sent back a short note saying he would answer me when he had time. Of course, I never heard from him again. He still regularly thrashes Christians, including yours truly. He once called me "the Godzilla of the Right."[65] Nice guy.

If there is hate existent in this debate over homosexuality, it appears to be coming from the other side. During the conflict in Colorado over the Amendment 2 initiative, I was the target of great venom. (Adopted by Colorado voters in 1992, the legislation forbade local governments from classifying homosexuals as a protected class of people in regards to employment and housing. Amidst bitter debate, it was struck down in 1996 and deemed unconstitutional in a condemning and outrageously worded opinion by the U.S. Supreme Court.) During that period, our buildings were spray-painted with bigoted slogans. We received death threats and telephone bomb warnings. Bloody animal parts were brought to the front of the headquarters building, and a mock funeral found its way onto our property. Vicious lies were told about us and publicized widely in the press. Throughout Colorado Springs and Denver, talk show hosts and newspaper reporters told local citizens that I had called each of the school superintendents in town and demanded the names of all homosexual teachers—so I could run them out of town.[66] Any thinking person would know that this was untrue, because schools cannot give personal information about a teacher, much less details of his or her sex life. It didn't matter because the story had "legs." Finally, the three superintendents here in Colorado Springs issued statements vindicating me.[67] But still the lies continued to spread.

These are the tactics, mind you, of the folks who accuse Christians of being hate-filled and intolerant. I will say it again: It is a game of intimidation and threats.

I share these stories to help you withstand the criticisms when they come your way, because they *will* come. If you have the temerity to confront the homosexual juggernaut, someone will attack your integrity. And when they run out of ideas, they will begin to shout. I've gotten used to the unfairness of these tactics (sort of) and have decided it goes with the territory. Do not get discouraged when it happens to you. Just hang in there and keep doing what is right. Remember, Jesus was unjustly accused, too.

AN UNHAPPY LIFESTYLE

At the risk of being misunderstood, let me acknowledge that there is a great reservoir of hatred in the world, and some of it unfortunately gets directed toward homosexuals. It is wrong and hurtful, but it does happen. Every human being is precious to God and is entitled to acceptance and respect. Each of us has a right to be treated with the dignity that comes from being created in the image of God. I have no desire to add to the suffering that homosexuals are already experiencing. In fact, it has been my intention to help *relieve* suffering by clarifying its causes and pointing to a way out.

Living as a homosexual is not as happy-go-lucky as is frequently portrayed in the entertainment media. This lifestyle is a prison that leaves many individuals feeling hopeless and abandoned by God, family, and society; many of these individuals desperately want to be free of their same-sex attraction and the struggles that come with it.

I am especially sympathetic to homosexual men who, as effeminate boys, were routinely called "fag" and "queer" and "homo" by their peers. The scars left by those incidents can last a lifetime. In fact, I'm convinced that some of the anger in the adult homosexual community can be traced to the cruel treatment these boys were subjected to at the hands of other children.

As Christians, we must never do anything to cause hurt and rejection, *especially* to those with whom we disagree emphatically. We certainly cannot introduce homosexuals to Jesus Christ if we are calling them names and driving them away. Believers are called to show compassion and love to those who would be our enemies. These people, some of whom seem hateful themselves, need to be welcomed into the church and made to feel accepted and appreciated. At the same time, we must oppose their agenda, which is harmful to society, to families, and ultimately to homosexuals themselves.

A few years ago, Focus on the Family launched an outreach called Love Won Out. This ministry presents dynamic one-day events that provide conference participants—gay or straight—information on addressing, understanding, and preventing homosexuality. Through this international outreach, Focus on the Family promotes the truth that homosexuality is preventable and treatable—a message routinely silenced today. Whether you are an educator, parent, or even a gay activist, Love Won Out offers information, inspiration, and above all, hope!

Overcoming homosexuality is incredibly difficult, and I will not minimize the anguish that can accompany the process of addressing the hurts and needs that surround it. Nevertheless, change does happen. We know of thousands of former homosexuals who have escaped from the lifestyle. It is exciting to hear them tell their life-changing stories. Two of these individuals, Mike Haley and Melissa Fryrear, are on our staff and speak at Love Won Out conferences.

Mike's story emphasizes the enormous impact fathers have on their sons—either for good or bad. Mike's father had great expectations for his son, centered around sports and hunting. When Mike responded with failure followed by disinterest, his father reacted in anger, mocking the boy and calling him names—sometimes in front of his adult male friends. These responses drove a wedge between Mike and his father, despite a deep-seated need for his dad's attention and approval.

At a key point in Mike's childhood, a male colleague of his father befriended Mike and offered the affirmation the youngster so desperately craved. This attention soon turned sexual, leading to his first foray into homosexuality. For twelve years Mike lived as a homosexual, experiencing the emptiness of one-night sexual encounters that left him feeling more like a commodity for consumption than a beloved and respected man.

Despite his growing unhappiness, Mike initially resisted the idea that homosexuals could change: He had tried before and it didn't work. He resigned himself to the fact that he was gay. But God had other plans, revealing His love for Mike through the diligent pursuit and friendship of a Christian man who demonstrated unconditional love and challenged Mike with God's truth about homosexuality. Eventually, Mike was led to Exodus International, a ministry for homosexuals who desire healing and transformation.

Today, Mike is a happily married father of two

boys, a published author, and a popular speaker on the topic of homosexuality.

Focus on the Family staff member Melissa Fryrear also found hope after homosexuality through the message of Exodus International. After ten years of living as a lesbian, Melissa says, a television program featuring Exodus encouraged her to turn away from homosexuality: "I watched and listened in total amazement as men and women shared how they had overcome homosexuality through their relationship with Christ. I had no idea there was anyone else who had made the decision to walk away from homosexuality."

Today, Melissa can see the roots of her same-sex attraction in early life experiences, including dynamics in the relationship with her parents, sexual molestation by a man, and sexual experimentation as a preteen. When she severed ties with her lesbian lover after turning to God for strength and renewal, Melissa had a new beginning; now she has a life-giving public testimony about the transforming power of Jesus Christ.

Mike and Melissa are two of thousands of individuals who are living proof that homosexuals *can* change. While that may sound like heterodoxy to those living in homosexuality, in reality people are turning away from same-sex relationships and resisting same-sex attractions through the power of Jesus Christ.

To summarize, I've tried to communicate in this chapter that we are obligated as Christians to treat homosexuals respectfully and with dignity, but we are also to oppose, with all vigor, the radical changes they hope to impose on the nation. It is vitally important that we do so.

With that in mind, let's talk about where we go from here.

5

HOW WE CAN WIN THIS WAR

Here's the question of the hour: How can we stop the imperious courts and rogue local officials from overriding the will of the people, who continue to oppose homosexual marriage by a wide margin?

There is only one answer: Congress and the state legislatures must pass a Federal Marriage Amendment to define this historic institution exclusively as being between one man and one woman.

That is the passion of my heart at this stage of my life. Seven times in the past few months I have joined more than fifty pro-family leaders in Washington DC to implore members of Congress to protect the family while there is still time. I'm told there is a brief window, now that the president has expressed his strong support, when passage of a Federal Marriage Amendment might be possible. Still, the opposition to an amendment is formidable.

Since Congress apparently lacks the will to use its constitutional authority to rein in the power of the courts, "we the people" must fight for an amendment to the Constitution that will do it for us. Let us never forget that our nation was founded in response to tyranny and oligarchy without representation. A constitutional amendment is one avenue for ensuring that kind of tyranny does not rise up today.

In a recent article published in *National Review,* Notre Dame law professor Gerard V. Bradley noted, "The only way to rein in this runaway Court is to change the supreme positive law: the Constitution. The Federal Marriage Amendment (FMA) would do that. It would impose upon willful judges and justices a limitation on their ability to redefine the family. The amendment would leave legislatures free to extend some benefits to nonmarital households. But courts could not."[68]

Granted, it is terribly difficult to pass a constitutional amendment under even the best of circumstances. It requires a two-thirds majority of both houses of Congress and passage by three-fourths of the state legislatures. That has only occurred twenty-seven times in our nation's history.[69] It will certainly not be easily accomplished at this juncture. As I write, thirty-four senators (seven Republicans and twenty-seven Democrats) are reportedly planning to vote against the FMA.[70] Nothing short of a national outcry by the citizens of this country will secure the necessary support.

Though imperfect, the Federal Marriage Amendment represents perhaps our last opportunity to ensure that traditional marriage is legally protected. The strength of the FMA is that it prevents the courts from distorting existing constitutional or statutory law into a requirement that marital status, or the legal incidents thereof, be reallocated pursuant to a judicial decree. In layman's terms, that means the FMA will ensure that the constitutional status of marriage is determined by the American people and their representatives, and not by unelected judges.

I know all too well that we face a daunting challenge. Even so, previous generations of Americans stayed the course when the nation was threatened, preserving our heritage despite overwhelming odds. The difficulties faced by our parents and grandparents in the Depression and World War II were staggering. Yet through their courage, resourcefulness, tenacity, and faithfulness to the task, the generations that followed have enjoyed unprecedented prosperity and blessing.

Now it is our turn. The peril we now face may not look the same as a world war or an economic depression, but it is every bit as ominous and formidable. The well-being of future generations depends upon the way we answer this threat. History will judge us on how we handle this crisis.

In a *National Review Online* article, Maggie Gallagher wrote, "Marriage is not an option, it is a precondition for social survival.... Winning the gay-marriage debate may be hard, but to those of us who witnessed the fall of Communism, despair is inexcusable and irresponsible."[71]

With God's help, and with a spirit of nationwide cooperation, I believe we can find the wisdom and strength to defend the legacy of marriage.

ALL HANDS ON DECK

I understand that you are very busy with your daily responsibilities. And the sheer import of this cultural challenge *can* be intimidating. Nevertheless, we need every hand on deck. This crisis is that important.

You may be outraged by the threat posed to marriage and family today, but emotions alone will not turn the advancing tide of the homosexual activist movement. Your concern and convictions must be translated into action. As Edmund Burke, the English parliamentarian, once said, "All that is necessary for evil to triumph is for good men to do nothing."[72]

The good news is that a substantial majority of the American people favor retaining the traditional and legal definition of marriage. In every state where voters have been asked to ban "gay marriage," they have done so by a stunning margin—69 to 31 percent in Hawaii,[73] 68 to 32 percent in Alaska,[74] 61 to 39 percent in California,[75] and 70 to 30 percent in both Nevada and Nebraska.[76]

But we need to work together. Maybe you would like to dive in and make a difference, but you simply don't know what to do. Here are some ideas for how you can help defend the legacy of marriage for generations to come:

- Contact your senators and representatives in Washington. Write a letter or place a phone call. I hear repeatedly that our leaders are not receiving public feedback regarding the Federal Marriage Amendment.
- Register to vote. Do it now in order to ensure that your voice will be heard during the next election.
- Take part in radio and TV call-in programs.
- Volunteer to teach a class or hold a seminar in your church, synagogue, or community to educate others about family-related issues.
- Put up lawn signs and distribute bumper stickers proclaiming the sanctity of marriage.
- Organize a debate in your community.
- Familiarize yourself with the realities of judicial tyranny. A good place to start is www.stopjudicialtyranny.com.

These are simply general suggestions for your course of action. There are hundreds more. A vast expanse of moral and legal territory is waiting to be reclaimed by concerned Americans like you and me, and we will accomplish that objective by taking one step at a time.

But we simply *must* have your participation in the struggle. Every person's involvement is critically important. There is no issue today that is more significant to our culture than the defense of the family. Not even the war on terror eclipses it. We must step up to the plate.

I am reminded of a personal story told by Dr. John Corts, former president of the Billy Graham organization. When he was sixteen, John and his younger cousins went to visit his grandfather's farm. They couldn't wait to get there and go out into the fields. They wanted to pitch hay and ride on the tractor. It sounded like so much fun.

But the grandfather was reluctant to let them go. They whined and begged until finally he said to John, "You are the eldest. You can take the kids to the field if you promise not to bring them back early. You must keep them out there until the end of the day."

John said, "I will do that, Grandfather." So they all climbed on the hay wagon and the tractor pulled them out to the field.

Very quickly, the kids grew tired and started

complaining. The work was hot and sticky and they were miserable. They began asking to go back to the house. But John said, "No, Grandfather told me to keep you out here."

By lunchtime they were exhausted and agitated. The hay was getting under their shirts and it itched. Everyone wanted to go home. But again John said, "No, Grandfather told me to keep you here."

About three o'clock in the afternoon, a large black storm cloud gathered overhead. The kids got scared and several were crying. "Please," they begged, "let us go home!" Still, the answer remained no.

At about five o'clock John said, "All right, it's time to quit." He loaded his cousins on the hay wagon, and they returned to the house. After they had taken their baths and been given something to eat, they rested for a while. Grandfather praised them warmly for the work they had done, and they became very proud of themselves.

That's when Grandfather told John why he didn't want them to quit early. He said, "This farm has been successful through the years for one reason: We have stayed in the field when we felt like coming in. We did what needed to be done, even when we wanted to quit. That is why I wanted the kids to have the satisfying experience of staying with something through the day."

Let me tell you what this story means to me.

We're in a very difficult situation now. It's tough. It's hard swimming against the tide of political correctness, the liberal media, the entertainment industry, Congress, the libraries, and the cultural forces making fun of us. It is not pleasant to be called "the religious right," "the far right," "religious extremists," and "fundamentalist right-wing crazies." None of us likes that. But being ridiculed and marginalized is the price we must pay to defend what we believe. Jesus told us that it would be that way.

God has called us to stay in the field till the end of the day, and I, for one, will do that as long as I have breath in my body. And I beg you to do the same. How can we remain silent when the next generation hangs in the balance?

If we persevere to the end, we will hear those wonderful words from the Father, "Well done, good and faithful servant!" (Matthew 25:21).

THE BATTLE BEGINS AT HOME

Let me offer one more word of advice. It is illustrated by an account of a battle described in the book of Joshua that occurred more than three thousand years ago. Joshua led a portion of his troops in a frontal assault of the Canaanite city of Ai. The Ai defenders came out in force to meet the Israelites, but they had been lured into a trap. The remainder of Israel's forces slipped in behind the enemy army and attacked the now-defenseless city. Ai's warriors looked back in shock and disbelief as they saw smoke rising from their burning homes.

Let's not let that happen with our own marriages and families. While we're out on the front lines engaging the enemies of traditional values, let's not allow our own homes, our own marriages, to go neglected or undefended. What good will it do to fight the foes of marriage in the city square while our own homes and families are collapsing from within?

The battle begins today, right now, under your own roof. If you have children, if you are married, or if you hope to marry, then while you are defending the cultural institutions of marriage and family, don't forget to defend and nurture *your own* marriage and family. Even if you are among those who do not have children and plan to spend the rest of your life as a single adult, it is in your own best interest to encourage and support families around you for the sake of your nation and its future generations.

We're sometimes tempted to believe that the battle at home is *against* our spouses and kids, but we must remember that we are charged with the responsibility to battle *for* them—for their protection, their moral character, their ability to engage the world around them, and their preparation to raise the *next* generation.

For all the strategies we have discussed for preserving marriage and the American family, perhaps our first and best defense of these cherished and vital institutions is to model healthy marriages and families for all the world to see.

Cultural conflicts such as this one require our attention, but we will lose the war if we lose the battle at home.

THE BATTLE BELONGS TO THE LORD

I will leave you with another story told in 2 Chronicles 32. There we read about King Hezekiah, who had served God wholeheartedly during his reign. However, he eventually faced a terrible crisis when Sennacherib, king of Assyria, invaded Judah with 185,000 well-armed and well-trained warriors. They wiped out the defenders of every city that lay in their path. Then they laid siege to Jerusalem and demanded that Hezekiah surrender or be destroyed.

These are the irreverent words shouted by Sennacherib to Hezekiah and his defenders, who were standing on the wall:

> "Do you not know what I and my fathers have done to all the peoples of the other lands? Were the gods of those nations ever able to deliver their land from my hand? Who of all the gods of these nations that my fathers destroyed has been able to save his people from me? How then can your god deliver you from my hand? Now do not let

> Hezekiah deceive you and mislead you like this. Do not believe him, for no god of any nation or kingdom has been able to deliver his people from my hand or the hand of my fathers. How much less will your god deliver you from my hand!"
>
> 2 Chronicles 32:13–15

Hezekiah and the prophet Isaiah did what you and I would have done under those distressing circumstances: They cried out to the God of Abraham, Isaac, and Jacob for deliverance.

Hezekiah also encouraged his countrymen with these inspired words: "Be strong and courageous. Do not be afraid or discouraged because of the King of Assyria and the vast army with him, for there is a greater power with us than with him. With him is only the arm of flesh, but with us is the LORD our God to help us and to fight our battles" (2 Chronicles 32:7–8).

And indeed the Lord did intervene as a result of the prayers of His people, delivering them from the hands of their enemies. That story should be of great encouragement to every believer who faces overwhelming odds at a time of great distress. We must go on our knees in concerted prayer, knowing that the God of Joshua and Hezekiah still hears and answers the petitions of His people. Ultimately, the battle belongs to Him and we are only His soldiers. *He* will defend the family, His great gift to mankind.

Let me emphasize that Focus on the Family will not waver during this time of national urgency. By working with other pro-family organizations and thousands of committed churches throughout the nation, we will strive to defend the principles that matter most. In so doing, we will likely be attacked, misquoted, and maligned by the liberal media and by those whose views on marriage and sexuality are radically different from our own. We covet your prayers during this time of intense debate. No matter what the odds, we are determined to stay the course. And may our Lord and Savior, Jesus Christ, bless us as we do.

Will you join me in this closing prayer?

Heavenly Father,
our great and magnificent King,
we ask You to intercede on behalf of the
institution of marriage and plead with You
to save the family from those who would destroy it.
With them is only an "arm of flesh,"
but our appeal is to the God of the universe
who has never lost a battle.
We do not deserve Your mercy,
but we kneel humbly before You today
and repent of our sin and disobedience.
When the history of this era is written,
let it be remembered as a time when
righteousness was rediscovered and when the
wickedness of this day would be transformed
by a nationwide spiritual renewal
that would sweep through the land.
For this, we and future generations
will be forever grateful.
Amen.

FREQUENTLY ASKED QUESTIONS ABOUT "GAY MARRIAGE"

Many people are confused by the arguments they are hearing in the media on this subject. Superficially, what the "gay marriage" advocates are saying may seem fair and logical. Scratch the surface, however, and you'll find that their assertions don't hold up. As you engage in conversation and debate with your friends and neighbors, please consider these answers to the following commonly asked questions.

Q: Isn't this a civil rights issue?

A: No. Civil rights is the shorthand way of referring to the struggle to overcome discrimination based on unchangeable physical characteristics, such as skin color or ethnic heritage. Homosexual activists often use this argument, but more and more black leaders are speaking out against it. In fact, the spokesman for the largest coalition of supporters for the Federal Marriage Amendment is Walter Fauntroy, a civil rights leader who marched with Martin Luther King Jr. in the 1960s.

Q: If we change the Constitution to say homosexuals cannot marry, isn't this discrimination?

A: Generally, the amendments to the Constitution define people's rights—the right to religious freedom, the right to bear arms, the right to vote at age eighteen, etc. The marriage amendment would simply define another right: the right to marry. It is discriminatory in the same way that the Constitution says seventeen-year-olds cannot vote.

Q: Shouldn't any two people who love each other be committed to one another?

A: Absolutely, and people do it all the time. But we don't necessarily call it marriage. There are many kinds of loving commitment that are not marriage. Friends are committed to each other, a parent is committed to a child, and grandparents are committed to their grandchildren. All these are forms of love. All of them require a commitment. None of those commitments is marriage.

Q: What's wrong with letting homosexuals marry?

A: Everything. Marriage is defined by the God of nature, and a wise society will protect marriage as it has always been understood. Marriage is the way our culture promotes monogamy, provides a way for males and females to build a life together, and assures that every child has a mother and father.

Q: Homosexuals can't produce children, but many male-female couples can't either. What's the difference?

A: This is the exception and not the rule. Many childless couples adopt, and this way their adoptive children receive the benefits of having both a father and a mother. It is impossible for a homosexual couple to bestow that benefit on any child, even if that couple adopts or uses artificial insemination.

Q: What about people who are too old to have children, even adopted ones?

A: The reason for supporting the institution of marriage is rooted not just in child rearing. Man and woman were made for each other, and the state has a compelling interest in supporting this undeniable and ancient truth.

Q: Isn't it true that what kids need most are loving parents, regardless of whether the parent is a mother or father?

A: No. Children need a loving mother *and* father. A wealth of research over the past thirty years has shown this. The most loving mother in the world cannot teach a little boy how to be a man. Likewise, the most loving man cannot teach a little girl how to be a woman. A gay man cannot teach his son how to love and care for a woman, nor can a lesbian teach her daughter how to love a man or know what to look for in a husband. Is love enough to help two gay dads guide their daughter through her first menstrual cycle? Unlike a mom, they cannot comfort her by sharing their first experience. Little boys and girls need the loving daily influence of both male and female parents to become who they are meant to be.

Q: But isn't it better for a child to grow up with two loving same-sex parents than to live in an abusive home or be bounced around in foster care?

A: You're comparing the worst of one situation (abusive heterosexual parenting) with the best of another (loving same-sex parenting). That's apples and oranges. Actually, research reveals that child abuse is at its lowest when children live with both biological parents, compared with higher rates for children who live with at least one non-biological parent or caregiver. Same-sex parenting situations make it impossible for a child to live with both biological parents, thus increasing his or her risk of abuse.

Q: Why don't gays have the same legal right to marry that heterosexuals do?

A: All people have the same right to marry, as long as they abide by the law. You cannot marry if you're already married; you cannot marry a close relative; an adult cannot marry a child; you cannot marry your pet; and you cannot marry someone of the same sex.

Q: Aren't homosexuals born that way? Isn't it therefore intolerant to prohibit them from marrying?

A: There have been many attempts by researchers to prove that homosexuals are born that way. None has proven the case. Most researchers conclude that homosexual tendencies are formed early in childhood and have to do with the failure of a child to bond with a parent.

Q: Isn't banning gay marriage just like banning interracial marriage?

A: Not at all! Being black or white, Hispanic or Asian, is not like being homosexual. The ban on interracial marriage was put in place to keep two races apart; that was wrong. Marriage is God's way, and society's way, of bringing two people together; that is right.

Q: But haven't we seen all kinds of family diversity in various civilizations throughout history?

A: No. Anthropologists tell us that every human society is established by males and females joining in permanent unions to build a life together and to bear and raise their children. The differences we see in family from culture to culture are primarily variations on this model: how long the male and female stay together, how many spouses either can have, and how the work is divided. But there has never been a culture or society that made homosexual marriage normative.

Q: How does someone's homosexual "marriage" threaten everyone else's families?

A: Gay activists are not asking for just one homosexual marriage, even though they often personalize it by saying, "Don't you interfere with my family, and I won't interfere with yours." What the activists want is a new national policy saying that having a mom and a dad is no better than having two moms or two dads. That policy would turn some very important principles upside down.

Marriage would become merely an emotional relationship that is flexible enough to include any grouping of loving adults. If it is fair for two men or two women to marry, then why not three or five or seventeen? The terms *husband* and *wife* and *mother* and *father* would become merely words with no meaning. Parenthood could consist of any number of emotionally attached people who care for a child.

Q: Even so, with so many divorces, traditional marriage doesn't seem to be doing all that well.

A: You're right. Marriage isn't working well. So what should we do? Erase the marriage laws? We have laws against murder, but people still commit murder. Do we erase the murder laws? Of course not. When laws aren't working, legislators try to fix them. We should work to strengthen marriage, and many are doing just that. High divorce rates are one result of another failed experiment from the liberal left: no-fault divorce. These laws make it much easier for a spouse to walk away from marital problems, rather than try to solve the problems. No-fault divorce has been a massive failure—children and parents have been hurt far more deeply than ever imagined.

The revolutionaries of the no-fault divorce movement claimed that the "till death do us part" portion of marriage wasn't that important. They were wrong. The same-sex marriage proposition claims that the "husband and wife" portion doesn't matter. Here we go again.

Q: Doesn't expanding marriage to include homosexuals actually help strengthen marriage?

A: Just the opposite. Recent evidence from the Netherlands, arguably the most "gay-friendly" culture on earth, reveals that homosexual men have a very difficult time honoring the ideals of marriage. A British medical journal reports that male homosexual relationships last, on average, eighteen months, and that gay men have an average of eight partners a year outside of their "committed" relationships. Contrast that with the fact that 67 percent of first marriages in the United States last ten or more years, and more than 75 percent of heterosexual married couples report being faithful to their spouses.

Q: Christians are called to show compassion and understanding. If it will bring happiness to homosexuals, why should we oppose gay marriage?

A: If someone is heading off a cliff, the compassionate response is to try to stop him, not allow him to fall and then offer to treat his injuries. It is the height of compassion for people of religious faith to unite to oppose this potential societal disaster—with its litany of pain and suffering—before it is too late. We have already seen that the media's positive portrayal of homosexuality has enticed many young people into this behavior. Should government sanction "gay marriage," many more will be drawn into this destructive lifestyle.

Developed by Glenn T. Stanton, director of social research and cultural affairs at Focus on the Family. Also by Pete Winn, associate editor of CitizenLink at Focus on the Family. This material has been adapted from the Focus on the Family booklet *Is Marriage in Jeopardy?* The full booklet, with citations, is available on-line at www.citizenlink.org.

HOW YOU CAN SUPPORT THE FEDERAL MARRIAGE AMENDMENT

I strongly encourage you to send a letter to Congress or to the editor of your local paper, voicing your support for the Federal Marriage Amendment. We've made it easy for you. Included in this section are all the talking points you will need to create a compelling letter.

You have heard, no doubt, the liberal argument against the Federal Marriage Amendment—that it will write bias and discrimination into the U.S. Constitution. That lie has been repeated loudly, and often, in the days since President George W. Bush came out in favor of such an amendment.

There's only one way to prevent your friends and neighbors from believing this lie: You have to tell them the truth.

Few ways of doing that are more effective than writing a compelling letter to the editor. That's why we've put together some key points that refute the liberals' argument, which we hope you will take a few moments to assemble into a letter to your local newspaper.

Here's how it works:

1. Look over the four sections below. From each section, select one paragraph and copy it into a text document. No matter which ones you choose, the result should be a finished letter of no more than 225 words.
2. Print out your letter and add your signature, making sure to include your name, full address, and phone number. Then mail it to your local newspaper, congressman, or senator.

Here are the selections from which you can assemble your letter.

Opening Paragraph (choose one)

- President Bush and other conservatives have been accused in recent weeks of seeking to "put bias in the Constitution" by endorsing an amendment that would define marriage as solely the union of one man and one woman. Nothing could be further from the truth.

- Liberals like Ted Kennedy and the *New York Times* editorial board have alleged in recent weeks that the Federal Marriage Amendment would "put bias in the Constitution" by declaring marriage to be exclusively the union of one man and one woman. It is a specious, deceptive argument.

- You've probably heard in the past few weeks the charge that the Federal Marriage Amendment, which would define marriage in the U.S. Constitution as the union of one man and one woman, would write discrimination into our country's founding document. Don't believe it for a second.

Second Paragraph (choose one)

- Gay marriage has never been a constitutional right in America or any other civilized nation. Those who support the amendment aren't trying to deprive homosexuals of any of the legal protections they currently enjoy; instead, they are trying to prevent runaway courts from creating out of thin air new "rights" that would prove detrimental to society.

- The truth is, the Constitution is going to be altered one way or the other. Either that change will come from unelected, unaccountable judges intent on creating a right of homosexual couples to marry when the Constitution grants no such right; or it will come from the American people through this amendment to preserve marriage as it has served society for millennia.

- It is not homosexuality, but marriage, that is under attack. Left unchecked, rogue judges intent on finding new rights in the Constitution will succeed (someday soon) in extending marriage benefits to gays. Supporters of a marriage-protection amendment aren't out to discriminate against anyone; they simply want to preserve the institution of marriage as it has served society for centuries.

Third Paragraph (choose one)

- Crying "discrimination" is not the only strategy liberals have unleashed to defeat this amendment, though. They also have argued that gay marriage is a civil rights issue akin to the African American struggle for equality. No less a civil rights icon than Jesse Jackson has denounced that claim, noting that "gays were never called three-fifths human in the Constitution."

- Amendment opponents have also turned to an emotional argument in asking, "How does one couple's gay marriage threaten anyone's heterosexual marriage?" This question misses the point: The goal of gay activists isn't the individual relationship of any two people, despite such statements; it is the revision of national policy to say that gender, especially in child rearing, is inconsequential, even though research indicates children do best when raised by a married mother and father.

- Amendment supporters have been disparaged as "bigots." How can that be, when the language being proposed is identical to the language of the Defense of Marriage Act, passed by 427 members of Congress? Are they—and former president Bill Clinton, who signed the bill into law—bigots, too?

Concluding Paragraph (choose one)

- These and other distortions of the truth must be resisted, because marriage and the benefits it brings must be protected.

- Don't fall for these manipulative arguments. Stand firm for the sanctity of marriage.

- This aggressive campaign to undermine marriage as it has always been known can be defeated—but only if we all stand up to support the Federal Marriage Amendment.

ORGANIZATIONS AND RESOURCES FOR THE CONCERNED CITIZEN

WEBSITES WITH INFORMATION ON SAME-SEX MARRIAGE

CitizenLink. "Same-Sex Unions and Parenting." See www.family.org/cforum/fosi/marriage/ssuap. This website of Focus on the Family offers helpful information defending natural marriage. Includes an up-to-date list of where each U.S. Senator stands on the Federal Marriage Amendment.

Family Research Council. See www.frc.org. For specific articles on "gay marriage," go to www.frc.org/file.cfm?f=KEYWORD&key=DP.

The Alliance for Marriage. See www.allianceformarriage.org. This group spearheaded the push for the Federal Marriage Amendment.

American Family Association. See www.afa.net. The AFA networks individuals and groups to promote pro-family policies and legislation.

BOOKS

Mike Haley. *101 Frequently Asked Questions About Homosexuality.* Eugene, OR: Harvest House, 2004. Former homosexual Mike Haley is manager of gender issues for Focus on the Family and chair of the board of Exodus International, the largest evangelical Christian ministry reaching out to those affected by homosexuality. In his book, Mike addresses questions pertaining to one of our nation's most divisive issues.

Glenn T. Stanton. *Why Marriage Matters: Reasons to Believe in Marriage in Postmodern Society.* Colorado Springs, CO: NavPress, 1997. Drawing from one hundred years of social science research, this book examines why traditional marriage and the family matter so much for children, men, and women in every important measure of human well-being.

Glenn T. Stanton and Dr. Bill Maier. *Marriage on Trial: The Case Against Same-Sex Marriage and Parenting.* Downers Grove, IL: InterVarsity Press, 2004. This book will help you make the case for natural marriage and explain why same-sex "marriage" is so damaging to our culture.

RELATED RESOURCES

CitizenLink: Focus on Social Issues. "Is Marriage in Jeopardy?" See www.family.org/cforum/fosi/marriage/faqs/a0026916.cfm. You may also request the article in booklet form (LF410) from Focus on the Family. Geared to help those engaging in the debate, this resource provides answers to some of the frequently asked questions about this cataclysmic social battle of same-sex "marriage."

Dr. James Dobson. "State of the Family: Spring 2004." *Focus on the Family*. This broadcast recording is available through Focus on the Family. Request audio tape B00015C for a $7 suggested donation or a CD version (B00016D) for a $9 suggested donation. As homosexuals are allowed to marry, what's to stop three women from marrying two men? Or a father from marrying his daughter? It sounds farfetched, but once the legal definition is expanded, traditional marriage and the family is on the road to collapse.

Dr. Bill Maier, Glenn T. Stanton, and Maggie Gallagher. "Why Does Marriage Matter?" *Focus on the Family*. This broadcast recording is available through Focus on the Family. Request audio tape CT590 for a $7 suggested donation or a CD version (CD293) for a $9 suggested donation. This two-day broadcast includes sensible arguments to use when explaining why marriage is best if it's a lifelong union between a man and a woman.

George W. Bush and Dennis Prager. "Marriage: A Cause Worth Fighting For." President Bush addresses this subject among other topics in an address to the National Association of Evangelicals. Dennis Prager is also featured on this tape discussing this vital subject. Available through Focus on the Family. Request audio tape B00051B for a $7 suggested donation or a CD version (B00052D) for a $9 suggested donation.

RESOURCES FOR ENGENDERING A COMPASSIONATE RESPONSE TO HOMOSEXUALITY

Exodus International. See www.exodus-international.org. Exodus International is the largest evangelical Christian outreach to those affected by homosexuality.

Love Won Out. See www.lovewonout.org. This ministry of Focus on the Family promotes the truth that homosexuality is preventable and treatable—a message routinely silenced today. Love Won Out one-day conferences are geared to inform, inspire, and offer hope for educators, parents, concerned citizens, and even gay activists.

National Association for Research and Therapy for Homosexuality (NARTH). See www.narth.com. This organization's primary goal is to make effective psychological therapy available to all homosexual men and women seeking change.

Pure Intimacy. See www.pureintimacy.org/gr/homosexuality. Pure Intimacy is a Focus on the Family ministry created to help individuals affected by sexual addictions and intimacy disorders.

NOTES

1. Edward Westermarck, *The History of Human Marriage* (New York: Allerton Book Company, 1922).
2. Stanley Kurtz, "The End of Marriage in Scandinavia," *Weekly Standard,* 2 February 2004, 27. (While not technically considered marriages, registered homosexual partnerships have been treated as the equivalent of marriage relationships in Scandinavia for more than a decade.)
3. Stanley Kurtz, "Death of Marriage in Scandinavia," *Boston Globe,* 10 March 2004, A23.
4. George Gilder, *Men and Marriage* (Gretna, LA: Pelican Publishing Company, 1986), 62–63.
5. Ibid.
6. Charles W. Socarides, MD, *A Freedom Too Far* (Phoenix, AZ: Adam Margrave Books); Marshall K. Kirk and Erastes Pill, "The Overhauling of Straight America," *Guide*, November 1987.
7. Robert H. Bork, *Slouching Towards Gomorrah: Modern Liberalism and American Decline* (New York: Regan Book, 1997).
8. Maggie Gallagher, "The Stakes," *National Review Online,* 14 July 2003.
9. Jeff Jacoby, "Gay Marriage Would Change Society's Ideal," *Boston Globe,* 6 July 2003, H11.
10. Ibid.
11. Lornet Turnbull and Patrick Coolican, "Two Sides of Gay-Marriage Debate Face Off at Safeco Field Rally: Event Draws 20,000 People," *Seattle Times*, 2 May 2004, A1.
12. Kathyrn Masterson, "Chicago Couples Take Wait and See Attitude," *Chicago Tribune*, 3 May 2004, A3; Mark Niesse, "Black Clergy Rally in Atlanta to Dispel Comparisons Between Civil Rights and Gay Marriage," *Associated Press,* 23 March 2004; Putsata Reang, "Two Thousand Evangelicals Rally Against Gay Marriage," *San Jose Mercury News*, 5 April 2004, A9; Ulysses Torassa, "Thousands Protest

Legalizing Same-Sex Marriage: Asian Americans, Christians Rally in Sunset District," *San Francisco Chronicle*, 26 April 2004, B1.

13. Peter Smith, "Church Backs Opposition to Homosexuality," *Courier-Journal*, 5 May 2004, A1.
14. Bruce Nolan, "Ban on Same-Sex Unions Is Defeated," *Times-Picayune*, 24 February 2001, A13.
15. Martin Walker, "Golden Tribute to Iron Lady," *Guardian*, 8 March 1991.
16. See www.family.org/cforum/extras/a0029774.cfm.
17. "A Look at What Lies Ahead in the United States' Debate Over Same-Sex Marriage," *Associated Press*, 17 May 2004.
18. See www.polybiblio.com/bud/18642.html.
19. Internal telephone audit conducted of the United States Senate in May 2004.
20. Deborah Rankin, "Taxes: Plans to Ease Marriage Levy," *New York Times*, 9 September 1980, D1.
21. "President William J. Clinton Delivers Weekly Radio Address," FDCH Political Transcripts, 5 August 2000.
22. David Popenoe and Barbara DaFoe Whitehead, "The State of Our Unions: The Social Health of Marriage in America," The National Marriage Project, Rutgers University, 1999, 2. See http://marriage.rutgers.edu.
23. Barbara Kantrowitz and Pat Wingert, "Unmarried, with Children," *Newsweek*, 28 May 2001, 46; "Nuclear Family Fading," *Gazette*, 15 May 2001, A1; Eric Schmitt, "For First Time, Nuclear Families Drop Below 25 Percent of Households," *New York Times*, 15 May 2001, A1.
24. Don Feder, "Meltdown of Nuclear Family Threatens Society," *Human Events*, 4 June 2001, 9.
25. Cheryl Wetzstein, "Federal Marriage Initiatives Seen as Cost-Effective," *Washington Times*, 3 May 2004, A3.
26. Family Law Act of 1969, ch. 1608, 1969 Cal. Stat. 3312 (repealed 1994).
27. David Popenoe and Barbara DaFoe Whitehead, "The State of Our Unions 2002: The Social Health of Marriage in America," The National Marriage Project, Rutgers University, June 2002, 22. See http://marriage.rutgers.edu.
28. Linda Greenhouse, "The Supreme Court: Homosexual Rights; Justices, 6-3, Legalize Gay Sexual Contact in Sweeping Reversal of Court's '86 Ruling," *New York Times*, 27 June 2003, A1.

29. Ibid.
30. Maria Hinojosa, "Massachusetts Court to Rule on Same-Sex Marriage," *CNN International Online,* 14 July 2003.
31. Pam Belluck, "Same-Sex Marriage: The Overview—Marriage by Gays Gains Big Victory in Massachusetts," *New York Times*, 19 November 2003, A1.
32. Pam Belluck, "Massachusetts Arrives at Moment for Same-Sex Marriage," *New York Times*, 17 May 2004, A1.
33. Ibid.
34. Elizabeth Mehren, "Massachusetts Legislature Moves to Bar Gay Marriage," *Los Angeles Times*, 30 March 2004, A1.
35. Steve Blow, "Gay Marriage: Why Would It Affect Me?" *Dallas Morning News,* 13 February 2004, B1.
36. Kurtz, "End of Marriage in Scandinavia," 27.
37. Pamela Manson, "Appeals Seek Polygamy Right: Green, Holm Challenge Convictions Based on Sodomy Ruling; Polygamists Challenge Convictions," *Salt Lake City Tribune,* 15 December 2003, C1.
38. Alexandria Sage, "Utah Polygamy Ban Is Challenged: U.S. Supreme Court's Sodomy Ruling Is Cited," *Associated Press,* 26 January 2004.
39. Ibid.
40. Ibid.
41. "The Supreme Court: Excerpts from Supreme Court's Decision Striking Down Sodomy Law," *New York Times,* 27 June 2003, A18.
42. Michael Kinsley, "Abolish Marriage: Let's Really Get the Government Out of Our Bedrooms," *Washington Post*, 3 July 2004, A23.
43. Ibid.
44. Judith Levine, "Stop the Wedding: Why Gay Marriage Isn't Radical Enough," *Village Voice*, 29 July 2003, 40.
45. Ibid.
46. Stanley Kurtz, "Beyond Gay Marriage," *Weekly Standard*, 4 August 2003.
47. M. Pollak, "Male Homosexuality," in *Western Sexuality: Practice and Precept in Past and Present Times,* ed. P. Aries and A. Bejin, 40–61, cited by Joseph Nicolosi in *Reparative Therapy of Male Homosexuality* (Northvale, NJ: Jason Aronson, Inc., 1991), 124–25.
48. A. P. Bell and M. S. Weinberg, *Homosexualities: A Study of Diversity Among Men and Women* (New York: Simon and Schuster, 1978), 308–9; see also Bell, Weinberg & Hammersmith, *Sexual Preference* (Bloomington, IN: Indiana University Press, 1981).

49. Many of these studies are either presented or represented in the following: David Popenoe, *Life Without Father: Compelling Evidence That Fatherhood and Marriage Are Indispensable for the Good of Children* (New York: The Free Press, 1997); Glenn T. Stanton, *Why Marriage Matters: Reasons to Believe in Marriage in Postmodern Society* (Colorado Springs, CO: Pinon Press, 1997); Ronald P. Rohner and Robert A. Veneziano, "The Importance of Father Love: History and Contemporary Evidence," *Review of General Psychology* 5.4 (2001): 382–405; Kyle D. Pruett, *Fatherneed: Why Father Care Is as Essential as Mother Care for Your Child* (New York: The Free Press, 2000); David Blankenhorn, *Fatherless America: Confronting Our Most Urgent Social Problem* (New York: Basic Books, 1994); Sara McLanahan and Gary Sandefur, *Growing Up with a Single Parent: What Hurts, What Helps* (Cambridge, MA: Harvard University Press, 1994); Ellen Bing, "The Effect of Child-Rearing Practices on the Development of Differential Cognitive Abilities," *Child Development* 34 (1963): 631–48; Deborah Dawson, "Family Structure and Children's Health and Well-Being: Data from the 1988 National Health Interview Survey on Child Health," *Journal of Marriage and the Family* 53 (1991): 573–84; Scott Coltrane, "Father-Child Relationships and the Status of Women: A Cross-Cultural Study," *American Journal of Sociology* 93 (1988): 1088; Michael Gottfredson and Travis Hirschi, *A General Theory of Crime* (Stanford, CA: Stanford University Press, 1990), 103; Richard Koestner, et al., "The Family Origins of Empathic Concern: A Twenty-Six-Year Longitudinal Study," *Journal of Personality and Social Psychology* 58 (1990): 709–17; E. Mavis Hetherington, "Effects of Father Absence on Personality Development in Adolescent Daughters," *Developmental Psychology* 7 (1972): 313–26; Irwin Garfinkel and Sara McLanahan, *Single Mothers and Their Children: A New American Dilemma* (Washington, DC: The Urban Institute Press, 1986), 30–31; Sara McLanahan, "Life Without Father: What Happens to Children?" Center for Research on Child Well-Being Working Paper #01–21, Princeton University, 15 August 2001; Paul R. Amato and Fernando Rivera, "Paternal Involvement and Children's Behavior Problems," *Journal of Marriage and the Family* 61 (1999): 375–84; David Ellwood, *Poor Support: Poverty in the American Family* (New York: Basic Books, 1988), 46; Ronald J. Angel and Jacqueline Worobey, "Single Motherhood and Children's Health," *Journal of Health and Social Behavior* 29 (1988): 38–52; L. Remez, "Children Who Don't Live

with Both Parents Face Behavioral Problems," *Family Planning Perspectives*, January/February 1992; Judith Wallerstein, et al., *The Unexpected Legacy of Divorce: A 25-Year Landmark Study* (New York: Hyperion, 2000); Nicholas Zill, Donna Morrison, and Mary Jo Coiro, "Long-Term Effects of Parental Divorce on Parent-Child Relationships, Adjustment, and Achievement in Young Adulthood," *Journal of Family Psychology* 7 (1993): 91–103.

50. For research on how marriage enhances adult well-being, see the following: Glenn T. Stanton, *Why Marriage Matters* (Colorado Springs, CO: NavPress, 1997); Linda Waite and Maggie Gallagher, *The Case for Marriage: Why Married People Are Happier, Healthier and Better Off Financially* (New York: Doubleday, 2000); Robert Coombs, "Marital Status and Personal Well-Being: A Literature Review," *Family Relations* 40 (1991): 97–102; I. M. Joung, et al., "Differences in Self-Reported Morbidity by Marital Status and by Living Arrangement," *International Journal of Epidemiology* 23 (1994): 91–97; Linda Waite, "Does Marriage Matter?" *Demography* 32 (1995): 483–507; James Goodwin, et al., "The Effect of Marital Status on Stage, Treatment, and Survival of Cancer Patients," *Journal of the American Medical Association* 258 (1987): 3125–3130; Benjamin Malzberg, "Marital Status in Relation to the Prevalence of Mental Disease," *Psychiatric Quarterly* 10 (1936): 245–61; David Williams, et al., "Marital Status and Psychiatric Disorders Among Blacks and Whites," *Journal of Health and Social Behavior* 33 (1992): 140–157; Steven Stack and J. Ross Eshleman, "Marital Status and Happiness: A 17-Nation Study," *Journal of Marriage and the Family* 60 (1998): 527–36; Robert T. Michael, et al., *Sex in America: A Definitive Survey* (Boston, MA: Little, Brown, and Company, 1994), 124–29; Randy Page and Galen Cole, "Demographic Predictors of Self-Reported Loneliness in Adults," *Psychological Reports* 68 (1991): 939–45; Richard Rogers, "Marriage, Sex, and Mortality," *Journal of Marriage and the Family* 57 (1995): 515–26. For research on how marriage enhances child well-being, see the following: David Popenoe, *Life Without Father* (New York: The Free Press, 1997); Glenn T. Stanton, *Why Marriage Matters* (Colorado Springs, CO: Pinon Press, 1997); Sara McLanahan and Gary Sandefur, *Growing Up with a Single Parent* (Cambridge, MA: Harvard University Press, 1994); Deborah Dawson, "Family Structure and Children's Health and Well-Being," *Journal of Marriage and the Family* 53 (1991): 573–84; Michael Gottfredson and Travis Hirschi, *A General Theory*

of Crime (Stanford, CA: Stanford University Press, 1990), 103; Richard Koestner, et al., "The Family Origins of Empathic Concern," *Journal of Personality and Social Psychology* 58 (1990): 709–17; E. Mavis Hetherington, "Effects of Father Absence on Personality Development in Adolescent Daughters," *Developmental Psychology* 7 (1972): 313–26; Irwin Garfinkel and Sara McLanahan, *Single Mothers and Their Children* (Washington, DC: The Urban Institute Press, 1986), 30–31; David Ellwood, *Poor Support: Poverty in the American Family* (New York: Basic Books, 1988), 46; Ronald J. Angel and Jacqueline Worobey, "Single Motherhood and Children's Health," *Journal of Health and Social Behavior* 29 (1988): 38–52; L. Remez, "Children Who Don't Live with Both Parents Face Behavioral Problems," *Family Planning Perspectives*, January/February 1992; Judith Wallerstein and Sandra Blakeslee, *Second Chances: Men and Woman a Decade After Divorce* (New York: Ticknor & Fields, 1990); Judith Wallerstein, et al., *The Unexpected Legacy of Divorce: A 25-Year Landmark Study* (New York: Hyperion, 2000); Michael Stiffman, et al., "Household Composition and Risk of Fatal Child Maltreatment," *Pediatrics* 109 (2002): 615–21; Nicholas Zill, Donna Morrison, and Mary Jo Coiro, "Long-Term Effects of Parental Divorce on Parent-Child Relationships, Adjustment, and Achievement in Young Adulthood," *Journal of Family Psychology* 7 (1993): 91–103.

51. California State Legislature Bills: AB 499 (1998), AB 537 (1999), AB 1785 (2000), AB 1931 (2000), AB 1945 (2000), SB 257 (2001). See www.leginfo.ca.gov/bilinfo.html.
52. Evan Halper and Carl Ingram, "Legislators Speed Through Final Bills," *Los Angeles Times*, 9 September 2003, B1.
53. Lynn Vincent, "Parliament OKs Law to Criminalize Speech Deemed 'Anti-Gay,'" *World Magazine*, 8 May 2004.
54. Ibid.
55. Rory Leishman, "Christians Right to Worry: Court Cases Show How Judicial Activists Have Destroyed Rule of Law," *Calgary Sun*, 8 May 2004, 15.
56. Robert Scheer, "More Vigorous Smut Prosecution Urged: Commission Asks Campaign but Three Members Reject Key Finding," *Los Angeles Times*, 17 May 1986, A1.
57. Michael Kirkland, "On Law: A Court for All Caesars," *United Press International*, 21 July 2003.

58. Fred Bayles, "Gay Marriage Ban Advances," *USA Today*, 30 March 2004, A1.
59. Kathleen Parker, "Marriage Clearly Requires Two Genders," *San Jose Mercury News*, 3 December 2003.
60. Deborah Mathis, "Anti-Homosexual Crowd Aided in Murder of Young Gay Man," *Tribune Media Services,* 15 October 1998.
61. Interview of Wyoming Governor Jim Geringer by Katie Couric, NBC's *Today Show*, 12 October 1998.
62. Judy Keen, "Hillary Clinton Suggests an Ongoing Conspiracy," *USA Today*, 28 January 1998, A1.
63. Peter Baker and John F. Harris, "Clinton Admits to Lewinsky Relationship," *Washington Post*, 18 August 1998, A1.
64. Frank Rich, "New World Terror," *New York Times*, 27 April 1995, A25.
65. Frank Rich, "Godzilla of the Right," *New York Times*, 20 May 1998, A23.
66. Steve Rabey, "Focus Haunted by 'The Rumor,'" *Gazette Telegraph*, 12 December 1992, A1.
67. Personal correspondence from superintendents Harlan Else, PhD, Thomas S. Crawford, EdD, and Kenneth Stephen Burnley, PhD.
68. Gerard V. Bradley, "Stand and Fight: Don't Take Gay Marriage Lying Down," *National Review,* 28 July 2003.
69. The United States Constitution. See www.law.cornell.edu/constitution/constitution.table.html#amendments.
70. "Gay Marriage Ban Amendment Appears Dead in U.S. Senate," *Politics1,* 1 March 2004. See www.politics1.com.
71. Maggie Gallagher, "The Stakes," *National Review Online,* 14 July 2003.
72. See www.tartarus.org/~martin/essays/burkequote.html.
73. Mark Stricherz, "Gay Marriage and Election: The Media Won't Mention It, but Polls Show a Winning Issue for the GOP," *Weekly Standard*, 5 April 2004.
74. Ibid.
75. Ibid.
76. Ibid.

LIFE—INTERRUPTED. FINDING BALANCE FOR TODAY'S DRIVEN FAMILIES.

Do you spend so much time driving your children to practices and programs that they feel more at ease in the family car than in your own home? Are you running in circles, tired and depressed, too busy to enjoy a good book, take a walk with your spouse, or read your toddler a bedtime story?

If so, you're not alone. Dr. James Dobson offers practical advice for burned-out parents. Be renewed as you find more time to enjoy life, to nurture your family, and to develop a meaningful relationship with the Lord.

—from Dr. James Dobson, the bestselling author of *Night Light for Parents* and *A Family Christmas*

Coming Fall 2004

www.multnomahbooks.com  www.homecountsonline.com

STRAIGHT TALK TO MEN

In this classic book, Dr. James Dobson shows the difference between the world's perspective and God's perspective of manhood, giving you the information you need to build a strong home.

ISBN 1-59052-356-3

STORIES OF THE HEART AND HOME

With these collected anecdotes from Dr. Dobson's bestselling books, you'll find more than encouragement—you'll discover how to deal with real adversity, thrive in your relationships, and live with peace and purpose.

ISBN 1-59052-371-7

PARENTING ISN'T FOR COWARDS

Let's face it, raising children is often difficult, especially in this shock-wave world. Dr. James Dobson helps parents navigate the passage from early childhood through adolescence.

ISBN 1-59052-372-5

LOVE MUST BE TOUGH

In this popular classic, Dr. Dobson offers practical solutions for holding your marriage together when it appears to be falling apart. The principles of respect and "tough love" can rekindle romance at home and restore your relationship.

ISBN 1-59052-355-5

NIGHT LIGHT FOR COUPLES

Night Light, a daily devotional for couples from Dr. James and Shirley Dobson, brings you personal, practical, and biblical insights that will renew your marriage—tonight and every night.

ISBN 1-57673-674-1

NIGHT LIGHT FOR PARENTS

Night Light for Parents, a daily devotional from Dr. James and Shirley Dobson, brings you personal, practical, and biblical insights to keep your kids pointed toward the path to eternity.

ISBN 1-57673-928-7

LOVE FOR A LIFETIME

A Gold Medallion winner for more than ten years, *Love for a Lifetime* has brought hope, harmony, and healing to millions of homes, giving men and women powerful insights for building lasting marital harmony.

ISBN 1-59052-087-4

CERTAIN PEACE IN UNCERTAIN TIMES

Fight violence, hunger, disease, and death—on your knees! National Day of Prayer Task Force Chairwoman Shirley Dobson shows you how to nurture a true and lasting lifestyle of prayer.

ISBN 1-57673-937-6